Into Deeper Grace

Roger Allen Cook

Into Deeper Grace
by Roger Allen Cook

Printed in the United States of America

ISBN 9781615797301

Cover Art: "Off With The Evening Tide" by Charles Vickery
Used with permission of Clipper Ship Gallery
www. clippershipgallery.com
Photography: Robert D. Walker

www.xulonpress.com

Acknowledgements

I express my deepest gratitude to my family for their encouragement of my writing and for the wonderful support of my school and church colleagues as well. To all the members of my church who provided me with so many inspirational story ideas I send special thanks. You have all allowed me to share your grace experiences with so many.

Table of Contents

Introduction

"Into Deeper Grace" is the second volume in a three volume series that began with a volume entitled "Sailing By Grace", and which will hopefully be followed by the title "Sailing Home—The Journey of a Lifetime". The analogy of our lives being like great sailing ships continues in this volume with stories designed to lead us to leave the shallows and safety of the shoreline and launch out into the depths of the open sea of God's grace. When we experience the wonderful grace of God in our lives, it is not long before we begin to scan the horizon with a desire to head out into a deeper relationship with Him. I am glad you have decided to come along for the journey.

Grace

Into Deeper Grace

Sailing into deeper grace is a concept that involves growing strong in our Lord and Savior Jesus Christ. The newness of spiritual life must move through stages of growth in each aspect of our lives. We must venture out from the shore of our salvation into the deeper things of the Word, of prayer, and of faithfulness. The framework of this idea is described in this work as a sailing ship that must leave the shallows for the open sea. These great ships are made to sail the great oceans of this earth and not stay docked in the port. We too must grow up in grace and launch out into the deep in our walk with the Savior.

Redemptive waves of grace
Meet the dry soil of our lives,
As a brand new life emerges
And spiritual growth thrives.

An exciting place of starting
At the beginning of a dream
With no real desire to leave—
Good thinking it would seem.

There is a perception of safety
In staying close to the shore.
The waves seem a little smaller
Where the surf ceases to roar.

With our feet still on the sand
And feeling somewhat secure,
We are hesitant to venture out
Where conditions appear unsure.

A call is etched upon the lives
Whose hearts have Christ in place.
"Don't be satisfied in the shallows
Time to sail into deeper grace."

It is a part of the Master's plan
To see each life grow in grace,
As we learn to depend on Him
Seeing life and faith embrace.

The decision to answer the call
Usually fearful at first thought,
Adds new dimension to our lives
As dependence on God is taught.

There will be storms involved
And billows mighty and strong.
The dangers of life will come,
But in Christ we can sail on.

There will be some heartaches
And disappointments in the task,
Yet obedience in the adventure
Is all that the Savior will ask.

Turn loose of what seems safe
For the shore is not your place.
Enthrone Jesus as your Pilot
And set sail into deeper grace.

Luke 5:4-10 Now when he had left speaking, he said unto Simon, Launch out into the deep, and let down your nets for a draught. And Simon answering said unto him, Master, we have toiled all the night, and have taken nothing: nevertheless at thy word I will let down the net. And when they had this done, they inclosed a great multitude of fishes: and their net brake. And they beckoned unto their partners, which were in the other ship, that they should come and help them. And they came, and filled both the ships, so that they began to sink. When Simon Peter saw it, he fell down at Jesus' knees, saying, Depart from me; for I am a sinful man, O Lord. For he was astonished, and all that were with him, at the draught of the fishes which they had taken: And so was also James, and John, the sons of Zebedee, which were partners with Simon. And Jesus said unto Simon, Fear not; from henceforth thou shalt catch men.

The Wounded Sparrow

Cymonne Pyles, a vibrant, active child who loved gymnastics, cheerleading, and singing, began having headaches half way through her eighth year of life. As the pain in her head occurred with more regularity, her doctor thought it might be of the migraine variety or perhaps stress induced. Her parents, Jeff and Debi, wondered how stress could be a problem with a child who had invited Jesus into her heart as Lord and Savior at the age of seven and seemingly enjoyed life so completely.

As time passed, the headaches worsened, resulting in a trip to the emergency room. That night the Pyles family began a journey that would lead them to Henry Ford Hospital in Detroit, Michigan and eventually to the St. Jude Children's Research Hospital in Memphis, Tennessee. Tests revealed that the headaches were caused by a malignant tumor in her brain called a Glioblastoma Multiforme. It was a malady that children rarely survived.

Her first brain surgery lasted for more than thirteen hours and the doctors said she probably should not have survived that experience. This was followed by numerous other surgeries, aggressive chemo and radiation therapies, and massive doses of steroids. Through it all she had an "I'm all right" signal with her dad. He would hold her hand when she came through a procedure and as soon as she was able, she would give it a squeeze. That always let him know that she was ok.

Although her life became filled with endless medical issues, Cymonne never lost her love of singing. In fact, on her way to surgery, with her head shaved and circles marked on her scalp, she would sing her favorite song for her doctors and nurses. The name of the song was "His Eye Is On The Sparrow" and the words below, by Civilla Durfee Martin, reveal how appropriately they applied to her situation.

Why should I feel discouraged, why should the shadows come,
Why should my heart be lonely, and long for heaven and home,
When Jesus is my portion? My constant friend is He:
His eye is on the sparrow, and I know He watches me;
His eye is on the sparrow, and I know He watches me.

Refrain
I sing because I'm happy,
I sing because I'm free,
For His eye is on the sparrow,
And I know He watches me.

She knew that she was a wounded sparrow that God had His eye on and she trusted Him with her whole being. One time when the misery index from all the treatments was pretty high, she told one of her favorite nurses that she wasn't afraid to die because she had Jesus in her heart. Although ready to die, she didn't want those who had fought so valiantly on her behalf to think that she had given up on the fight. Later, Debi and Jeff would remember that conversation the nurse had related to them.

In March of 1998, shortly after her 10th birthday, she began to show signs of a recovery that caused some to think that her condition might not be terminal. Sadly, by late April she was once again off to the emergency room with extremely labored breathing. In triage, her breathing returned to normal and her eyes opened with a look of astonishment, as if she was looking out into deep space and she said "Mom." She then collapsed and stopped breathing. Medical personnel were able to revive her, but she had to be placed on a ventilator in intensive care. She had to be heavily sedated to keep her from fighting against the intrusive machinery that was helping her breathe. This left her in an effectively paralyzed condition.

The doctors told her parents that although she couldn't move, she could still hear them. As they watched her laying there in her bed, helpless, with all that medical apparatus just barely keeping her alive, they knew in their hearts that it was time for them to let her go. That was when her parents tenderly whispered to their little child how proud they were of her and the way she had fought this enemy that had attacked her body. They told her that if it was the Lord's time for her to go, it was ok. At that moment a little hand squeezed her father's hand for the last time as she signaled to him, "I'm ok." Within one minute of that squeeze, on April 28, 1998, a little wounded sparrow flew like an eagle, higher than ever before, all the way to Jesus. She now knows from personal experience that He truly did have His eye on her all the time.

If you know Him, He has His eye on you too. God's grace is a wonderful thing!

More Grace

There is something mentioned in the Bible that is better than grace, I told our church people. That thing to which I was referring is, more grace. I linked God's grace to the manna He provided for His people as they wandered in the wilderness and like that manna, grace needs to be received each and everyday. Yesterday's grace was specifically designed for the needs of that time, and tomorrow more grace will be provided to match all the situations of life that we will face. Reach out today and get as much grace as you need, because the price has been paid in full and your account balance is unlimited.

On considering the rising of the sun
And the dawning of a brand new day,
I see that familiar enemy pacing
Who desires to make me his prey.

He has many shapes and illusions
From my flesh to that old serpent himself,
Seeking to facilitate my downfall
With methods of subtlety and stealth.

I know that I cannot hope to win,
For my strength only knows how to fail.
Tossed and confused by harsh elements,
I buckle under as life's storms assail.

I need from my Heavenly Father
Another portion of sustaining grace
To defeat the temptations of today
That will challenge me face-to-face.

More grace my prayer will request—
More grace poured upon me each day,
More grace from the heart of my Savior,
More grace to lead me all the way.

On considering the rising of the sun
And the dawning of a brand new day,
"Oh gentle Shepherd—It's me again,
More grace, more grace—I pray."

James 4: 6 But he giveth more grace. Wherefore he saith, God resisteth the proud, but giveth grace unto the humble.

The Covering of Grace

Protections against the harsh elements of life are important for our physical well-being. In many ways we provide these physical needs for those we love. Spiritually speaking, however, our needs for protection can only be provided by God's grace. What a blessing it is when we allow Him to cover us by His grace and then use us as an instrument of His covering for others.

As the bitter winter wind howls
And the snow whirls and blows
A young mother covers her child
From toes to the tip of his nose.

So carefully providing protection
From the elements that surround,
She shares the warmth of her heart
Setting a pattern so very profound.

For love of family a man labors,
Involved in the daily grind of life,
Providing the financial covering,
For his children and for his wife.

Attentive to ever-present dangers,
A watchman with a spiritual eye
For an enemy who would devour,
And every deceitful temptation try.

They are pictures of an eternal truth—
The love provision Jesus set in place.
Righteous robes purchased at Calvary,
Our God's perfect covering of grace.

We are covered in life, and in death
Since His sacrifice has set us free;
Mercy granted by a humble prayer,
Covered by God's grace eternally.

Psalm 32:1 Blessed is he whose transgression is forgiven, whose sin is covered.

A Miracle of Grace

It was a beautiful Michigan fall morning and after dropping her son off at school, she drove over to the shopping center to meet the girls for breakfast. She arrived a little early for their meeting, so she parked her car near the restaurant and decided to walk along the sidewalk and do some window shopping.

She was lost in her own little world when she walked by a passageway that led between the stores and back to the service side of the mall. In an instant, the entire course of her life changed as a man emerged from the shadow and violently grabbed her. She was absolutely stunned as he dragged her down that passageway to a loading dock at the back of the building and brutally raped her.

He finished his despicable act and ran off, leaving her dazed and in shock. One of the worst things that she could ever have imagined had just happened to her. It seemed surreal, almost like it was happening to someone else while she watched. As soon as she was able, she jumped to her feet and fled back down the passageway, and across the parking lot to her car.

She drove home and immediately got into the shower and attempted to wash away the evil that had just been done to her. As she stepped out of the bathroom, she began to tremble uncontrollably and realized that she was in shock and desperately needed help. She called her husband who came home immediately and together they spent the rest of the day involved in a visit to the police station and the indignities of emergency room procedures endured by rape victims. He found himself as helpless to ease her pain as he was to deal with the rage deep within him toward the criminal who had hurt his wife.

To some, it might seem like the worst of this tragic situation was over, but that was not the case. The next five years of their lives were an unmitigated disaster. Denial, panic attacks, self-punishment, thoughts of suicide, doctors, counselors, and prescription drugs were all a large part of these tragic years. Depression dominated her life.

Her husband tried to be supportive, but she pushed him away. She truly wanted to die. She worked hard to make her husband hate her so he wouldn't be hurt by her death. Life got so difficult that a trial separation was attempted. Eventually their relationship fell into a state of hopelessness that brought them to a mutual decision that divorce was the ultimate fate of this damaged marriage. How sad for a couple that had been so in love just a few years before!

As they planned the initial steps of their divorce, her heart screamed out that it was not what she really wanted. That was when she remembered meeting her brother's pastor. She had visited his church once to see the baptism of her niece, and now wondered if he might be of help in this desperate hour. She made a contact and met with Pastor Tom, at the church the next day. Her husband had encouraged her to go, but he privately held little hope that anything would change.

The solution to five years of personal suffering was found that day when she heard about how God loved her and truly understood her pain. She gave her life to Jesus and asked Him to help her. So began a miracle of God's Grace. The tragedy that had occurred five years earlier had taken her to the edge and caused her to despair of continuing her life, but she found out that living in God's grace was the answer. She left the church that day a new person. The peace of God filled her heart and she knew it. She couldn't wait to tell her husband what had happened.

He noticed this change in her when he got home. They actually sat down and talked together without the conversation ending in an argument. He felt the hand of Grace reaching out to him and agreed to attend church with her the next Sunday. He wanted to see for himself just what this change was all about. He had given his life to Jesus many years earlier, but drifted far away from that decision. There was spiritual work that needed to be done in his heart too.

The church began to minister to them through God's word and the small group ministry. They came back to see Pastor Tom as a couple and this miracle of Grace continued. The anger and bitterness that had disabled them for the last five years was gone. Their marriage became a blessing once again, as their love for one another exploded to a whole new level.

On the next two anniversary dates of their tragedy, they had to battle a difficult sense of edginess and the anger that attempted to intrude into their relationship. They realized that there were still some fears and feelings that needed to be faced. As the eighth anniversary of their tragedy approached, the Lord spoke to their hearts. They approached Pastor Tom with an idea and an unusual appointment was made.

The three of them met at the shopping center, on the tragic anniversary date, at the exact time in the morning that she had been attacked eight years earlier. They then proceeded to retrace the steps she had walked on that fateful day. They walked along the sidewalk past the stores, down the passageway, and over to the loading dock at the back of the building. On this day, there were workers present who watched in curiosity as one by one each of them prayed. A husband and wife offered prayers of thanksgiving for their journey from depression, from strong anti-depressant drugs, from thoughts of suicide, and from plans to divorce, to a new life in God's grace.

On that special day, the last of the chains of a family tragedy were cast into the ocean of God's amazing grace. Isn't the grace of God a wonderful thing?!

Hebrews 4:16 Let us therefore come boldly unto the throne of grace, that we may obtain mercy, and find grace to help in time of need.

An Appointment with Grace

I am thankful that the Savior came and found me just like He did this man named Zacchaeus. My appointment with grace has paid great earthly dividends and guaranteed eternal blessings. If you have not previously kept your appointment with grace, right now would be a great time.

He resided in a town in Judea
Well known in the area around.
You see, he collected their taxes.
His methods were often unsound.

At times more was taken than due.
Mercy would never be put in place.
His profession, one that was hated—
Yet he had an appointment with grace.

He heard about a special prophet
Who was going from town to town,
Healing and changing many lives
With multitudes crowding around.

Being a man of shorter stature
He climbed into a sycamore tree,
To raise himself above the crowd,
For this Jesus he wanted to see.

As the Savior passed that way
He called Zacchaeus to His side:
"Make haste and come down here
For in your house I will abide."

God met that day with a sinner,
And a life was totally changed.
Wrongs would be made right
And all life patterns rearranged.

You might not be a tax collector
But you know the meaning of sin,
And the need for emancipation
From the fear that rules within.

Come and meet with the Savior.
Invite Him to stay at your place.
Salvation will come to your heart
Through an appointment with grace.

Luke 19:8-10 And Zacchaeus stood, and said unto the Lord: Behold, Lord, the half of my goods I give to the poor; and if I have taken any thing from any man by false accusation, I restore him fourfold. And Jesus said unto him, This day is salvation come to this house, forsomuch as he also is a son of Abraham. For the Son of man is come to seek and to save that which was lost.

Chosen by Grace

They shake their heads in humble awe when they talk about how God is using them in His service. I am referring to people who were very active in their sin and rebellion when God broke through to their wandering heart. God's great forgiveness often leads to situations of great usefulness. I have said before that great sinners often make great servants when their hearts are turned from the world back to God. Those who have been greatly forgiven make excellent watchmen and mentors to warn others not to walk in their footsteps and experience the heartache of grievous sin first hand.

When closely I examine my heart
And the specific failures that I see
My mind just can't help but wonder,
"Why would God's grace choose me?"

I'm convinced God knew the future
And the footsteps that I would take—
The oft chosen path of my rebellion
And each and every fleshly mistake.

Yet in His providence He chose me
To be named as His adopted child.
He lovingly allowed the Holy Spirit
To then help me become reconciled.

That is simply the nature of grace
As His love reaches those undone,
And then by no merits of our own
He gives us peace through His Son.

Consider now God's call on your life,
For He has saved you a special place.

Accept His invitation with your heart.
You're the winner—chosen by grace.

I Peter 2:9 But you are a chosen generation, a royal priesthood, an holy nation, a peculiar people; that ye should show forth the praises of Him who hath called you out of darkness into his marvelous light:

Hungry for Grace

There are times when I don't get to eat dinner when I was expecting to and my body quickly reminds me that it is being deprived. There is a spiritual banquet set for us in God's word everyday and so often we choose not to stop and eat. It may be necessary for us to ask God to rekindle our hunger for His grace in our everyday lives. If you ask for His help in this matter, His grace will boost your appetite and provide lunch too.

The desires of this life are many
And of numerous type and sort.
Some of them are obviously evil
While others are of good report.

At times desires that are good
Can be inappropriately used.
When their function is distorted
Designed purposes are abused.

The craving and need for food,
A common and necessary drive,
Nourishes our physical bodies,
And allows us to remain alive.

Nourishment to the extreme
Can change a good thing to bad
As health begins to deteriorate
Thus making the latter days sad.

The longing for personal love
Is a need which must be met,
But within a framework of honor
That the Holy Scriptures have set.

If Spiritual life has come inside
And all priorities have changed,
The hungers of a redeemed heart
Will be supernaturally rearranged.

Are you really hungry for grace
And the movement of God's hand
When He redirects your journey
In ways you don't understand?

Then regularly eat God's word.
Take its precepts deep within.
You can't get too much grace,
But You can get too much sin.

Matthew 5:6 Blessed are they which do hunger and thirst after righteousness: for they shall be filled.

Rescued by Grace

Jesus came to this world to look for and save lost sinners. Aren't you grateful that His mercy and grace found you? Don't forget to tell Him of your gratefulness and show Him with your obedience to His word.

It always seemed so natural
To cut out, duck out, and run
From the pursuance of Grace
And inevitable confrontation.

Knowing the convoluted status
Of my rebellious attitude
My mind sought only to cope
And His judgments to elude.

As He pursued this wayward one
I ran faster in the other direction.
Miserable to the nth degree
My heart resisted correction.

His patience exceeded my sin
As the burden of failure grew.
His Spirit whispered deep inside
And I knew what I had to do.

As I turned and ran toward Him,
I saw forgiveness in His face;
And by the mercy offered that day,
I was lovingly rescued by grace.

Matthew 18:11-13 For the Son of man is come to save that which was lost. How think ye? if a man have an hundred sheep, and one of them be gone astray, doth he not leave the ninety and nine, and goeth into the mountains, and seeketh that which is gone astray? And if so be that he find it, verily I say unto you, he rejoiceth more of that sheep, than of the ninety and nine which went not astray.

Ripples of Grace

Alden Toney was a member of the Gilead Baptist Church for many years and also served on the staff as our director of music. Some years later, after he retired and moved to Florida, he had a most amazing experience.

He had traveled to Cleveland, Tennessee to hear his granddaughter present her senior music recital at Lee University. The Sunday following the recital he attended the worship service of a large church in town. As he listened to an evangelist give the morning message, he was totally surprised when the man specifically took note of his presence and asked to talk with him after the service. Alden had traveled with the Toney Brothers Quartet for many years, and it was not unusual for him to be recognized by people who remembered his contralto tenor voice.

When they met after the service the evangelist introduced himself and told Alden that he looked very familiar. Through a series of questions he discovered that Alden had spent most of his adult life in the Detroit area and that he had served as Music Director at Gilead. During those years the church had reached out to their community by running one of the largest bus ministries in the country. Children by the tens of thousands had been transported to Sunday school and church by a fleet of blue buses with signs on the side that read "Gilead Baptist Church, We Love Kids." Over the years, thousands of bus kids had trusted Jesus as their personal Savior. The evangelist looked at Alden and said, " Now I know why I recognized you. I was one of your bus kids." The buses were named after the cartoon characters painted on the side and he even remembered the name of the bus he had ridden.

What an amazing thing it was to see first hand some of the spiritual fruit of Gospel seeds planted years earlier! This man had been contacted by Gilead as a boy, trusted Christ, and now years later he was preaching the Gospel to thousands of people all over the country. It appears that God gave us a view into what His grace can do when we are faithful to present the words of life to those around us. What bus driver or bus captain could have known that when they pulled up to a house so many years ago and picked up a kid for Sunday School, there would be such wonderful and eternal results?

Pastor Russ Grubaugh, the Director of Bus Ministries in those days, has received numerous reports about previously unknown details of how God has blessed the efforts of the people of Gilead and the outreach ministry of the blue buses. If we remain willing to put our hands into service for the Lord, He will continue to use those actions for His glory. Remember that we won't learn of all the results of ministry in this life, but when we see Jesus face-to-face He will give us "the rest of the story". In the mean time special glimpses of the ripple effect of grace are always a welcome blessing. Isn't God's grace a wonderful thing?!

The Author of Grace

The grace of God is a special thing that is somewhat difficult to define. It has been described as God's unmerited favor, while others define it as the divinely given ability to do anything that pleases God and brings Him glory and honor. You could attempt to select the perfect definition, but your choice would ultimately be insufficient to truly and completely describe it. We do know that God provides it to us at His own expense and that the price of grace was paid in full at Calvary. When we see Him face to face, I want to learn first hand what grace is really all about.

The creation of this old world—
In just one week it was finished.
But when the pair elected to sin
The future was sadly diminished.

God had given Adam the law—
Just one rule had to be followed.
We all know how long it lasted
After the bites were swallowed.

This caused a great dilemma—
Now mankind was facing death
And separation from a holy God
When they draw the last breath.

The one true remedy available
That could close this eternal gap
Was this new thing called grace
And the redemption it would tap.

Making the law wasn't difficult
God simply set the truth in place,
But it was a very different matter
When it came to paying for grace.

It was God who invented grace,
But the price was extremely high.
For the true cost to be paid in full,
Our Savior had to willingly die.

Now God dispenses grace freely
Because Calvary paid for it all,
Providing for eternal salvation,
If on the name of Jesus we call.

Everyday grace—His is available
As the circumstances of life arise.
Whether through failure or in a trial
Grace comes in just the right size.

God's grace came into my life
Long before I even knew its name.
It purchased me and changed me,
And I will never again be the same.

Where do you stand with grace—
Inside Christ or outside the gate?
Its benefits are awaiting your call.
Dial now—no good reason to wait.

Romans 5:19-21 For as by one man's disobedience many were made sinners, so by the obedience of one shall many be made righteous. Moreover, the law entered, that the offense might abound. But where sin abounded, grace did much more abound; That as sin hath reigned unto death, even so might grace reign through righteousness unto eternal life by Jesus Christ, our Lord.

The Foundation of Grace

From the owner to the architect to the project manager, you will find that there is a great interest in the foundation of a new structure. Life has taught them that foundation problems can be very expensive to repair and can actually put the entire project at risk. We are warned by Scripture to take heed to the foundation that we build our lives upon.

Our lives are like a building,
Stone upon stone put in place.
The question is what to build on.
Will it be a foundation of grace?

The cornerstone of the structure
Must bear the entire weight
Of all that our lives entail,
Laid upon it at a daily rate.

Jesus is that true foundation
Who can bear the days in sum—
Each action and each mistake,
The pain that surely will come.

Many have attempted to build
Their foundation upon the sand
But as the rains of life came
They found it could not stand.

The foundation of grace was tested
When God asked His Son to endure
The judgment of every individual,
With a payment strong and sure.

Upon this tested and solid base
We can frame the walls of days
And decorate them by His grace
As we learn of His perfect ways.

As strong storms come upon us,
And they most definitely will,
Our structure is covered by grace,
And our fear His love will still.

Some of the parts of your building
Will be burned up and pass away,
But other parts will be purified
And will shine for an eternal day.

When the final inspection is made
And with fire He tests each deed,
The foundation will be unmoved,
By our God forever guaranteed!

Build your life on this foundation.
Put pure building materials in place.
On this Rock that will never move—
God's wonderful foundation of grace!

1 Corinthians 3:9-11 For we are laborers together with God: ye are God's husbandry, ye are God's building. According to the grace of God which is given unto me, as a wise masterbuilder, I have laid the foundation, and another buildeth thereon. But let every man take heed how he buildeth thereupon. For other foundation can no man lay than that is laid, which is Jesus Christ.

The Lighthouse of Grace

When I was young I used to listen to a gospel quartet sing a song entitled *The Lighthouse.* As I think about the words to that song I am reminded that there are still so many who are lost on the dangerous journey of life, not having found the peace that is provided in the harbor of God's grace.

We were sailing down the coast.
The weather was extremely rough.
Knowing there was danger ahead,
Strained senses were not enough.

Historically ships had been lost
To the points of rock and reef,
When unexpectedly they found
Total disaster with no relief.

Into this precarious situation
Our charted course had led,
Looking for that safe harbor,
Somewhere in the journey ahead.

Weather continued to be a factor
As the air moved off the shore
And over cooler ocean waters.
Visibility was limited and poor.

All hands were on high alert,
Eyes straining to pierce the murk,
Ears listening for telltale sounds,
The helmsman tense as dangers lurk.

Then leeward off the ship's bow
Quite a distance out into the mist,
Something that looked like smoke—
A ghostly scene some would insist.

Now echoes the sound of a horn
And a beam comes into our view—
The welcome beacon of a lighthouse!
All hands knew exactly what to do.

Adjusting our direction to avoid
Peril that the warning conveyed,
We turned the corner toward home
With joy in our hearts displayed.

Jesus said we are like a lighthouse
That must warn this world of sin,
And the sacrifice that the He made
So their hearts can invite Him in.

His grace and mercy are waiting
In the harbor His arms provide.
Let the Lighthouse of Grace direct,
And come sailing safely inside.

John 12:46 I am come a light into the world, that whosoever believeth on me should not abide in darkness.

The Stewardship of Grace

When you serve the Lord, you should not always expect to be allowed to see the results of your actions. We are to plow and plant and then understand that God will determine when and where the increase is shown. Every now and then, God opens a door and gives us a glimpse of the results of our efforts. Those glimpses are very blessed and encouraging moments. Imagine how wonderful it will be one day when God reveals the entire results that He reaped from our service.

I remember so clearly the day
God gave me a brand new heart.
He covered it with His grace
And its reborn beat did start.

He said, "This heart is Mine.
My son has paid the total price,
And now I have loaned it to you
With some very important advice.

"I am a very expectant Master
Who, putting an investment in place,
Requires His servant to practice
The stewardship of grace."

Someday the Master will return
And in His presence we will bow.
The records will all be examined—
What we did, and when and how.

Were we faithful to re-invest
The grace He placed in our care,
Touching the hearts of others
And planting grace seeds there?

Or were we unprofitable servants
Selfishly withholding our stash,
Soaking up all available blessings
And hoarding them like carnal cash?

When grace received is dispensed,
Put to work in the Kingdom cause,
An amazing transaction takes place
Explained in multiplication laws.

Invest the grace given to your life
In the heart and life of another.
Then, an eternal, spiritual return
Is the reward you will discover.

God will permit you to witness
His grace when it's multiplied,
Through the efforts of His child
Whose labor has been sanctified.

Oh, child of God, don't be weary.
Step forth, reach out from the heart.
Invest His grace in your actions.
Today is a great time to start.

1 Peter 4:10 As every man hath received the gift, even so minister the same one to another, as good stewards of the manifold grace of God.

Too Busy for Grace

I am reminded of past family gatherings and all the details that had to be arranged. It is easy to get overwhelmed in the doing of a thing and end up too busy to enjoy the event. In serving the Lord, we can get so caught up in the activity that we don't have time to stop and worship God. Let's allow God's grace to help us keep a spiritual perspective in all we do.

In the midst of loving service
With so many things to do,
Details that need attention,
Two hands just seem too few.

The desire to meet each need,
The planning of every stage,
Dominates our consciousness
And all the faculties engage.

It is the proper thing to serve,
To see each event done right;
But as physical strength fails,
Sincere motives fade from sight.

One was heavily encumbered
With the service of the hour
When the Lord came to visit
And display His heavenly power.

The plan, though well intentioned,
Soon had her flittering about.
She tried to do what was required
But just ended up burned out.

"Lord, my sister is simply sitting
At your feet in stillness there
Please tell her I need some help.
She just doesn't seem to care."

His reply—"Slow down Martha.
Your efforts are not in vain.
But she is teaching a lesson
And making eternal truth plain.

"Sit down here with me for awhile
And listen to the truth of my voice.
While serving is always important,
Time with me must be first choice."

Lord, teach us to daily meet You—
To rekindle Your love deep inside,
So our service will be Spirit-filled
And Godly fruit will forever abide.

Luke 10: 38-42 Now it came to pass, as they went, that he entered into a certain village: and a certain woman named Martha received him into her house. And she had a sister called Mary, which also sat at Jesus' feet, and heard his word. But Martha was cumbered about much serving, and came to him, and said, Lord, dost thou not care that my sister hath left me to serve alone? bid her therefore that she help me. And Jesus answered and said unto her, Martha, Martha, thou art careful and troubled about many things: But one thing is needful: and Mary hath chosen that good part, which shall not be taken away from her.

Times of Sadness

All of Her, All of Him

The Prayer

The Morning Song

Dying Grace

Greg's Broccoli

A Parent's Prayer

Sure Hope—No Hope

Only Yesterday

Suddenly Alone

The Grace of Life

The Call

The Winds of Sorrow

When Someday Became Today

All of Her, All of Him

My mother was the secretary of her church for over thirty years and was well known for her Godliness and sharp memory. She spent the last decade of her working life teaching typing, shorthand and business courses at the Christian school where I am the administrator. She walked with the Lord on a daily basis and was constantly leaving me notes about a special discovery she had made in her study of the Bible. The last year she taught, we began to see problems with her short-term memory and by the end of the year we knew that something was wrong. That something was Alzheimer's disease. She has gradually slipped into a mental fog that has robbed her of the ability to speak or do things that require a sequence of steps. Although she cannot presently read her Bible or utter a simple prayer, I believe her communion with her Lord is in a language that cannot be written with mortal pen nor spoken by mortal tongue. God is near to her through this earthly trial and will bring her to the home He has prepared for her in the time He has chosen. He does all things well.

She had the sharpest of minds
With a memory clear and strong.
In latter years it began to fade,
Showing something was wrong.

Having given so many years
Of faithful service to her Lord,
Difficulties were hard to accept.
Symptoms couldn't be ignored.

The simple steps in a sequence
Became a challenge to complete.

The diagnosis was confirmed
As faculties started to retreat.

Then stepped forward a hero.
His love empowered by grace,
As he met the needs of his wife
By giving her care first place.

"There is nothing I will spare
In money, effort, and attention
For this one I love so deeply.
This is my solemn intention."

He cooks and cleans and attends
To her personal needs and more.
His tender patience displayed
But Only more hardship in store

Oh what a disheartening disease!
It takes away the use of the mind
And one's ability to know and do,
Leaving such limited use behind.

God's grace is always available
As we face the hardships of life,
And a husband joyfully commits
To the long term care of his wife.

How long will his strength last
As the burdens continue to rise.
The years and his health will tell-
None of us can really surmise.

For now, her sweetness shows
Though her future might look dim.
While Alzheimer's has all of her,
Blessedly, she has all of him.

God knows all about these things
And the difficulties they imply.
His great love has a perfect will.
Only He has the answer to "Why?"

Now, her communion with the Lord
Cannot be written with mortal pen.
Someday she will have a new mind
And she will never struggle again.

Redeemed so many years earlier
When she invited the Savior within,
Soon Alzheimer's won't have any of her,
And she'll forever have all of Him.

Isaiah 46:4 And even to your old age I am He; and even to gray hairs will I carry you; I have made, and I will bear; even I will carry, and will deliver you.

The Prayer

I was describing her desperate condition to my pastor, after the service one Sunday when he solemnly asked me, "Have you prayed *the prayer*?" I knew exactly what he meant. His compassionate question touched me deeply. Pastors seem to have a way of doing that.

Mom had been suffering from Alzheimer's disease for more than ten years, and the continuing progress of the malady was devastating. Her ability to speak had been gone for some time, and she had been forced to depend on facial expressions to communicate. Now even that was gone as was almost any ability for independent movement, leaving her in need of total care. My dad was always the first in line to serve. He spent hours each day patiently coaxing his beloved wife to eat and take in fluids. He always told people, "She would have done this for me if the circumstances were reversed."

Having gone from a delightful woman of great mental acuity to a non-communicative, almost comatose patient was a dramatic descent. Now she had stopped eating and rarely opened her eyes. She had made a pact with Dad when she was first diagnosed that no extreme measures would be allowed to artificially prolong life as her condition deteriorated. No feeding tubes or breathing assistance would be employed to prevent her earthly exit. Dad was committed to this agreement, but found that keeping it was a gut wrenching experience.

That Sunday, I left speaking with my pastor, and went to the nursing home to join my father at her bedside. Even in an unconscious condition, she was beginning to show grimaces of pain. I asked dad if he was ready to give her up, and pray *the prayer*. He understood ramifications of what I was saying. This is a man who had committed his finances, his time, and most importantly of all, his physical health to her care. He had a real concern that he wouldn't live long enough to see his mission through to the end. Little did he understand how close his arduous work would take him toward his own physical collapse.

He responded to my question by saying that he was ready to pray *the prayer*. Seeing her suffering and deteriorating condition had finally moved him to let go of that which he had worked so hard to keep. On that Sunday, around noon, we prayed (my father, my wife, and I) and asked God to take the one we loved so much to heaven, if it was His will. We had no idea how God would respond to that heartfelt request, but we had prayed *the prayer* with sincerity and all due gravity. We knew that God does all things well, and this situation would be no different.

On Monday morning I went back to the nursing home to check on her condition and see Dad, before teaching my class. I work at a school within walking distance of the nursing home. After a short visit I crossed the room intending to go back over to the school, but could find no freedom in my spirit to exit. It was as if God spoke to my heart and said, "Don't leave." I removed my coat, returned to her bedside, and waited.

As the time passed, my memory painted wonderful experiences of the past on the canvas of my consciousness until I noticed that her breathing had slowed. A nurse came by to check her pulse and found it to be very faint. She told us that mom could linger for days or even weeks in this condition. Dad knew there was a problem, he later told me, because her hand was growing colder. I sensed the difficulty of the situation and began mentally noting the widening time between her labored breaths. It was only a few minutes later that my mother stepped out into eternity. She exhaled her last earthly breath and immediately inhaled her first breath of Heaven.

Twenty one hours after we prayed *the prayer*, God took her home. He gave her dying grace, when the time was right. He gave my dad comforting grace for pain that can only be felt by one committed to a lifetime of loving and caring for another. And yes, real men do cry.

I thank the Lord, for answering *the prayer* and allowing me the privilege of witnessing the last moments of one of the Godliest women I have ever known. The experience makes me want to shout out loud—"Isn't God's grace a wonderful thing?!"

In loving memory of Ludie Cook

The Morning Song

I will never forget my mother's faithfulness to meet with the Lord every morning to pray and read His word. Meeting with God when the day is new is a special and blessed activity. If you set aside time to meet with Him, He will never miss the appointment.

She sang a sweet song to Jesus
Each morning around His word.
He rearranged the earthly chords
From the humble notes He heard.

Such a tender song about her love
Of a Savior who was always near
Giving direction to the daily path
For this child He loved so dear.

Her song was about her children
And the family that she knew best,
The ministry she labored to serve,
Her many friends, and all the rest.

Her singing wasn't without flaw—
She knew she was saved by grace
And that her sins had been forgiven,
Washed away without even a trace.

One sad day the questions began,
As her thinking became confused,
And she needed help and guidance
With almost everything she used.

Her last struggle of life was intense.
Gifted faculties continued to erode.
As loving hands faithfully attended
Sharing with her a most difficult load.

Now a special morning has dawned.
There is a heavenly song she can sing.
On a cloudless and never-ending day
She is praising Him for everything.

I was tempted to sing the song of grief.
Death can inspire our sorrow to abide.
But instead I'll sing the morning song
And like her, place God's word inside.

Psalm 5: 3 My voice shalt thou hear in the morning, O Lord; in the morning will I direct my prayer unto thee, and will look up. In memory of my mother, S. Ludie Cook

Dying Grace

As we get older and experience the loss of some of those we dearly love, we tend to more often consider eternal things. I sometimes wonder what it will be like to close my eyes on Earth and get my first glimpse of Heaven. That is where my finite mind shorts out and I am reminded that I cannot even imagine how wonderful it will really be.

There is a place quite special
That only by death can we see,
Where the physical passes away,
And the temporal meets eternity.

For the present, faith is required;
And sight will just have to wait.
These earthly eyes cannot see
Celestial visions inside the gate.

The mysterious jumping-over point
That sometimes causes us to fear,
With grace so desperately needed
As the crossing time grows near.

One wonders what it must be like
To simply reach out and touch
That special thing called eternity
Of which we have heard so much.

Our first breath of celestial air,
A glimpse of the Savior's face,
Are wonderful heavenly benefits
Of this thing called dying grace.

Open your heart to His saving grace,
And faithfully use it to live every day.
Then the end becomes the beginning
When, "Come home," you hear Him say.

Hebrews 9:27-28 And as it is appointed unto men once to die, but after this the judgment: So Christ was once offered to bear the sins of many; and unto them that look for him shall he appear the second time without sin unto salvation.

Greg's Broccoli

The room was quiet as loved ones waited all around. The terrible illness that so savagely attacked his system had taken its course. The respirator had been removed due to a loss of brain function and Greg's father laid his ear to his son's chest and waited. He listened to his last heartbeat and through his tears announced, "That's it, he is with Jesus now". And so it was that on November 11, 2000, at 10 years of age, Gregory David Price left us and entered the presence of his Lord and Savior, Jesus Christ.

I remember Greg in many ways; from his birth to the day I became his first principal in school. I cherish a special memory of him as a young child when he visited my home and discovered my garden. You see, he was a committed broccoli devotee and was amazed to see the stuff in its original agricultural state. This event occurred near the end of the growing season that summer in Michigan.

I promised him that the next season I would grow a row of "Greg's Broccoli" that would be exclusively reserved just for him. He never let me forget that promise. In the spring he was looking for broccoli even before it was time for planting. Once we did get those plants in the ground, this three year old couldn't hardly wait for them to grow. He would check on the progress of his broccoli each week at church or whenever he would see me.

What a joy it was to see him that summer standing by the garden with a large head of broccoli in each hand, held up in a victory stance. The simple pleasure of watching a child realizing the good feeling that comes at the time of harvest is one that will be treasured always. It is needless to say that Greg visited his plants several times that summer to continue the harvest of his beloved broccoli.

Some might think that Greg was just a tender plant that didn't live long enough to bear fruit, but I beg to disagree. Greg loved the Lord and prayed for friends and neighbors that they would come to love God like he did. He was given a gift of life that was only ten years in length, but he used that gift to God's glory. His life was a blessing to all who knew him.

If you have a child or grandchild or even a youthful neighbor or church kid, enjoy every moment of their youth that you can. We are not promised more than today and the precious moments it provides. The Bible tells us that life is like a vapor that is here for only a little time and then vanishes away. We would all do well to use our lives as fully as did this little boy.

The following poem was written with thoughts of families like Greg's who have children who are extremely ill and face similar struggles.

A Parent's Prayer

Written with thoughts of Kyle, Kevin, Greg, Libi and all children and their families who face major childhood illnesses and disabilities. It is amazing how God uses them to bless our lives with their love and remind us of how much for which we have to be thankful. Do you know of a family in these circumstances who needs you to faithfully remember them in prayer?

Dear Lord, I need Your help.
As You know my child is ill.
My heart is heavy within me.
I come now seeking Your will.

You have given him to me
Showing Your grace so plain.
I know You want the best for us
Even when I witness his pain.

Oh, God, my child is so fearful
Of doctors and tests and such.
Though I desire to help him
I find I am afraid just as much.

He tries to understand it all
And just why he must endure.
He looks to me for comfort,
But I can't provide the cure.

You know all about suffering
Watching Your Son on earth,

Bleeding and dying for our sin,
Providing for the new birth.

Give me strength in this crisis
As I stand by my ailing child,
To hold him while he is crying
With arms so loving and mild.

Please send to us each hour
A touch of Your special grace,
And help my son to trust You
In all the trials we face.

Hold his hand, hold his heart,
This tender lamb so small.
Oh, lead us Gentle Shepherd,
And love us through it all.

II Corinthians 12:8-10 For this thing I besought the Lord thrice, that it might depart from me. And he said unto me, My grace is sufficient for thee: for my strength is made perfect in weakness. Most gladly therefore will I rather glory in my infirmities, that the power of Christ may rest upon me. Therefore I take pleasure in infirmities, in reproaches, in necessities, in persecutions, in distresses for Christ's sake: for when I am weak, then am I strong.

Sure Hope—No Hope

Funeral services can be somewhat similar to each other or they can be dramatically different. The manner in which the deceased lived life greatly influences the atmosphere of funeral viewing and the final service.

The man of God enters the room.
The sad call has come for his care.
There is a family clustered together,
And old friends have gathered there.

He considers just what he will say
About the one who here lies in state,
To comfort the hearts of the grieving
Whose weight of sorrow is so great.

He remembers the life surrendered,
How Jesus had been given first place.
With every act of sin forever forgiven
And eternal life guaranteed by grace.

Separation by death is a painful event,
But the Christian has a very sure hope,
That all who die in Christ are with Him,
Offering a peace that helps us to cope.

At times the preacher's task is harder
When the status of the heart is unclear,
And not knowing if this crossing over
Gave good reasons for anyone to fear.

What can he say when there is no hope
For God's saving grace was rejected?
The time for this decision was missed,
Now the penalties must be expected.

While life still courses within your veins
There remains open a window of grace.
Ask Jesus to provide for everlasting life
And make your funeral a hopeful place.

I Thessalonians 4:13-18 But I would not have you ignorant, brethren, concerning them which are asleep, that ye sorrow not, even as others which have no hope. For if we believe that Jesus died and rose again, even so them also which sleep in Jesus will God bring with him. For this we say unto you by the word of the Lord, that we which are alive and remain unto the coming of the Lord shall not prevent them which are asleep. For the Lord himself shall descend from heaven with a shout, with the voice of the archangel, and the trump of God: and the dead in Christ shall rise first: Then we which are alive and remain shall be caught up together with them in the clouds to meet the Lord in the air: and so shall we ever be with the Lord. Wherefore comfort one another with these words.

Only Yesterday

Nobody said it would be easy, and it wasn't. I wish someone could have come along and whispered special words of truth that would have made the pain go away, but they could not. The death of a loved one is something we all must learn about by experience. It is a path of life that must be traveled step by step. Isn't it wonderful to know that the One who took that great sacrificial journey to purchase your salvation will also walk with you through the painful valleys of life.

Wasn't it really only yesterday
That our life seemed so secure?
Then a most horrible phone call.
Now this painful grief to endure.

Suddenly, unchangeably, gone
It seems like my heart will break.
They say that this hurt will pass—
I wonder how long it will take.

Calls to family must be made,
All the questions they will ask.
A tough job someone must do—
It is my loving and solemn task.

My loved ones begin to gather,
Their sorrow is part of my pain.
I desire to offer them comfort,
But my words are often in vain.

My dearest is in Your care, Jesus,
From this life having been set free.

Hold us both near to Your heart
Until the time that You call for me,

Psalm 116:15 Precious in the sight of the LORD is the death of his saints.

Remembering Effie Haneline—A gracious Christian woman

Suddenly Alone

Death within a family can be devastating and much more so if the situation is sudden and unexpected. Turmoil within the heart and between family members is often a result of this type of tragedy. In these special circumstances God's grace is desperately needed and liberally provided.

Suddenly alone—what happened?
This is not how my life was planned.
Unsure about things I used to know,
My broken heart does not understand.

In anger I ask the question—"Why?"
It seems that I need someone to blame.
In spite all of the doctors' best efforts,
No one answers when I call her name.

What about the future of our children
And the various needs that they show?
What can I do to encourage their hearts?
How can I help to soften the blow?

A turmoil of spirit rages from within.
Fear, uncertainty—will they ever cease?
I cry out loud when no one is looking.
How will I ever find a lasting peace?

Gradually my heart begins to realize
Never, no never, was I left all alone.
God's merciful love was ever on duty.
His faithfulness was so clearly shown.

My arms and my life feel very empty.
Gone to Jesus is my loved one so dear.
Now God's holy presence fills my soul
As He tenderly teaches me not to fear.

I sense His special touch on my family
At every table, and each event to abide,
Bringing the peace only Jesus can give
And a comfort that reaches deep inside.

Today's pain will someday seem far away
As I allow His grace to rebuild my dreams,
And change the sadness of these solo notes
Into His symphony of a thousands strings.

Deuteronomy 31:6 Be strong and of a good courage, fear not, nor be afraid of them: for the LORD thy God, he it is that doth go with thee; he will not fail thee, nor forsake thee.

The Grace of Life

The hospital room seemed so small, so crowded, so sad. My heart broke as I watched a mother weep for her premature newborn daughter who lay dying just a few feet away. With a heavy heart and eyes that were hung with tears, I watched a tearful young father attend to his grieving wife. I saw brothers and grandfathers, all of them strong men, weep for the loss of the child. I saw the women of the family ministering to everyone in the room. Ella Grace Pfeifer was born with physical problems that were incompatible with life, and she lived for only a few precious minutes. I felt the close presence of the Lord in the room that day. I know that they all needed His touch. I know that I did too.

A few days later, friends and relatives came to the funeral to show their love and support for this young couple. I did my best to speak words of truth and comfort and God's love, but I realized that only God's grace, applied over time, could meet their needs. I watched as the family gathered around a small, white casket in a quiet cemetery. They knew that the love of a family was an important component of the healing process and they were ready to do their part. I purposed to try to be a part of that encouragement to them whenever the Lord gave me the opportunity. Hebrews 4:16, tells us, *Let us therefore come boldly unto the throne of grace, that we may obtain mercy, and find grace to help in time of need.* This tragedy would certainly qualify as a circumstance of great need.

Today, fourteen months later, I stand rejoicing at a bedside, watching that same young mother lovingly cradle her newborn daughter, who was delivered four hours before I arrived. The child is petite, (approximately 6 lbs.) with the prettiest red hair you could ever want to see. She fusses and her lower lip quivers a bit, bringing a soft response from her mom. The proud father then reaches out and securely scoops up this little infant with two strong but gentle hands. What a wonderful scene to witness! I gave a soft welcome and a blessing to Ava Grace Pfeifer, the child that God sent to fill the arms of a couple who have been dreaming of this day for a long time. On the inside my heart shouts, "Isn't God's grace a wonderful thing?!."

The Call

In the time of crisis and trouble, one of our first thoughts is, "Where can I get someone to help me?" One of the genuine blessings of this great country of ours is the fact that we do have emergency and military professionals who are dedicated and committed to public safety and national defense. Sadly, this high and special calling sometimes requires the ultimate sacrifice of health and even life itself. Too often these heroic efforts occur in the absence of expressions of gratitude from those who are being served.

The alarm call rings out on a dreadful day.
"Look up at the horror and come right away!
The need is so great, lives hang on the edge."
"We offer ourselves," is their sworn pledge.

Sirens sound out as heroes swing into action.
Though peril abounds, there is no retraction.
Reaching out for others and giving their hand,
They stand in the gap and die where they stand.

They rush in to rescue while others rush out.
The pathway of safety so rarely their route.
Danger rides with them each and every day.
"The security of others first," is what they say.

It does not take long for our heroes to die,
Leaving many loved ones who wonder why.
Speak up, you patriots. Speak up and shout!
Sacrifice and courage are what it's all about.

Stand up, thankful citizens of this nation great.
Give honor to all who have entered God's gate.

To those who continue in faithful service today,
When you next greet them, what will you say?

II Samuel 1:23, 25...In their lives and in their death they were not divided: they were swifter than eagles, they were stronger than lions. How are the mighty fallen in the midst of the battle!

Dedicated to all the American heroes of 9/11, of history, of today and of tomorrow.

The Winds of Sorrow

We live in a world that is filled with troubles and heartaches. Our sin made these things a regular part of life. When the storms of life blow your way, you will find protection and comfort from God's faithful presence.

When the storms of life are raging
And the winds of sorrow blow,
Relief is not found in endurance
But in peace that you can know.

A peace that comforts the heart
When the words of men just fail,
As waves of grief come crashing
And on the shore of the mind assail.

When your logic and understanding
Cannot begin to adequately explain
Those bitter tears flowing down
And the questions that rise again,

Remember that nature's Master
Whom the winds and waves obey
Would never leave you all alone—
Ever on duty each night and day!

He understands your heart's sorrow
From the storms that come and go,
And He covers your life with grace
When the winds of sorrow blow.

There have been many others
When troubled by tempests strong,
Who cried out for their Master
And did not have to wait long.

His comfort is expressly specific,
And His peace meets every need.
He stills that inward turbulence
When His precious Word we read.

Heartaches will paint your horizons,
Yet true wisdom you will show
By seeking shelter in His presence
When the winds of sorrow blow.

Psalm 30:5 For his anger endureth but a moment; in his favour is life: weeping may endure for a night, but joy cometh in the morning.

When Someday Became Today

It was a beautiful fall day as the warm sun burned off the morning chill. I arrived, left the parking lot, and entered the school building. The faculty meeting would begin in a few moments, and there were things to be done. Soon the majority of the three hundred plus cars that shuttle children to our school would be entering the parking lot and dropping their precious cargo at designated locations.

The day began with the faculty meeting where we discussed items of immediate importance and some of long-range significance. I dismissed the meeting with prayer and headed for our individual assignments with the energy and freshness that comes from a new day in a still new school year.

I proceeded to analyze those areas that needed my attention, and began to prioritize my work. This is a time of day that I make myself available on an impromptu basis to students, teachers, parents, etc. It is a busy period that settles down with the start of classroom instruction.

The day was progressing smoothly when at approximately 11:15 a.m. my secretary tracked me down and advised that Corporal Michelle Marshall of the Taylor Police Department had requested to meet with me and was waiting in the school office. Michelle was assigned to the youth division, and her presence meant something out of the ordinary was involved. I had worked with her on several other occasions and always found her to be very well adjusted to a position that required well-blended measures of firmness and compassion.

My instincts were on double alert as she requested that she and I meet privately in my office where she asked me about one of our first-grade children Diane Driskill. "There has been a problem at the home," she said as she inquired if we could supply any information we might have on problems within the family. As I brought the records in for review, my mind raced through various scenarios. After the record was reviewed, and found it to be devoid of any pertinent information, I asked Michelle the nature of the problem. Her response involved the most devastating statement I have ever heard. Diane had been killed by her grandmother only a few moments earlier. As shock flooded my soul, thoughts of my words spoken to the faculty in meetings past, rushed to my consciousness. “Someday we will lose one of our little ones, and the opportunity we have to work with them will be gone. We need to make diligent and wise use of the opportunities we have to love them and teach them and share our lives with them. Someday we will lose one, and we will need to know that we did our best with the responsibilities God gave to us." With the sudden violent discharge of a shotgun on that fall morning, “someday” became today. We could do no more for Diane; what was done already would have to suffice.

Michelle said that it appeared that the grandmother had killed her, and then turned the gun on herself. Although the attempt at suicide left her seriously wounded, the grandmother had called the police and reported what she had done. Later I would learn that the grandfather was also involved, and tried to take his own life at work.

I called my secretary Carol to my office. She informed us that she had talked to the grandmother earlier that morning, and had been told that Diane was ill and wouldn't be in school that day. She had known this lady for years and had always felt that little Diane was the most precious thing in her grandmother’s life. Carol was visibly shaken.

I determined at that point not to inform our staff in general, but only key members who could be of help immediately. I called Diane's first grade teacher to the office, and informed her that there were police concerns about the home, and asked if she could be of any help. She had called the home herself that morning and was told that the child was ill. I excused her, telling her not to worry, but to keep our meeting confidential. She would later thank us for not telling her the facts until later that afternoon.

After the police left, I called my administrative team together to discuss possible steps of action. My main concern was the children, in light of the fact that we had been warned that this tragedy would very likely be on the evening news (which turned out to be true). I wanted to provide information to the children to help them understand the situation, and wanted to alert the parents to the need for close attention to and support for their children. It was decided that a sealed letter would be prepared and sent home with each child in Diane's class. This would at least give minimum information to the parents. I asked my elementary principal to write the letter and see the task through while "keeping a lid on the situation". We also alerted as many parents as possible and asked them to arrive at school early, because we had to inform the class about a tragedy, and their presence in the room would be a great help. I arranged for the director of our daycare to be present since she had known many of the children for several years.

Thirty minutes before the end of school I called the teacher into my office and informed her of the tragedy. In her grief she recalled a conversation she had with the grandmother earlier that morning, trying to see if there had been any clues that could have alerted her to action that might have prevented this tragic loss. The best comfort for her broken heart was the memory of having recently prayed with Diane as she invited Jesus into her heart as her personal Lord and Savior.

With just a few minutes left in the day, I spoke to all the students in Diane's first grade class. I told them that Diane had died at her house that day, and had gone to Heaven to be with Jesus. Our Biblical belief tells us "to be absent from the body (in death) is to be present with the Lord for evermore." I asked if any of the children had lost grandparents or others in their families (many had). Then I told them it was okay to be sad or even cry, because we would miss her, but we knew beyond a doubt that she was with Jesus, and He is taking care of her now. I prayed with them, and asked God to help them understand, and asked that the Holy Spirit would comfort their hearts. I prayed for Diane's family and their hour of deep distress—that God would comfort them. The children would return the next day to find Diane's desk and her belongings had been removed. I had discussed this with the teacher who agreed that this action would help the class as they tried to go on with their lives.

The last few minutes of the day were gone, and the children left. I wondered if we had met their needs, and if we could have done a better job. God's grace was sufficient in those closing minutes of the day as sorrow was followed by a deep sense of peace. God does all things well. I believe it, and I trust Him.

Grace was certainly sufficient for that day, but the next day would require another dose. The story broke, and everyone wanted to talk about what happened. I determined that the school would have to make a statement. The news media was already clamoring for an interview with me, the teacher, and even students. I wrote a statement, and had it printed along with Diane's picture, and sent it home with the students
.

I informed our staff that I, alone, would be available for comments. They later thanked me for protecting them. Having one designated spokesman for the organization is a part of most policies involving crises.

Dealing with the media was an experience I could have done without. I realize their job is to "get the story behind the story," but along the way sensitivity and concern for the people involved is often discarded. There was more to the story, but I was determined that they would not get it from me. I said what I knew to be true, and what I believed to be appropriate. When the story broke, it was given a great deal of media coverage.

Several days later we buried Diane on a cold and rainy day. As I spoke to those who gathered at the service, I reminded them of the concern that Jesus has shown for the little children. When the disciples had determined that Jesus was too busy with adults to be bothered with children, He rebuked them saying, "Suffer the little children to come unto Me, for of such is the Kingdom of God." I said, "As she passed from life to death to eternal life, the Savior took her into His arms and carried her into eternity." As Isaiah said, "He shall gather the lambs with His arm, and carry them in His bosom." We said goodbye to Diane that day, but her memory remains and will always be a part of us.

It was later determined through psychiatric examinations that the grandparents were suffering from the rare disorder, “folie a deux,” a shared paranoia. They somehow had become convinced that there was an abduction conspiracy involving a neighbor, organized crime and the General Motors Corporation. They loved their granddaughter so deeply that they were willing kill her to keep her from being kidnapped and tortured. Both the defense and the prosecution agreed that they were insane at the time of the murder, and they were subsequently found not guilty by reason of insanity in Wayne County Recorder’s Court and committed to a psychiatric facility for treatment. They have since been released.

Someone has said that childhood is a season of growth and the prime time to plant the seeds of faith through which God will provide a harvest. Someday the time of sowing will be past. Those of us who have been given the opportunity to plant spiritual seeds in the lives of children must be faithful, so that when someday becomes today we will have no regrets. We will one day fully understand that those sown seeds will produce graceful results long after the last wave of time has broken on the shore of a measureless eternity.

Remembering

A Little Hand

The Captain

A Message from Heaven

Granny with a Red Dress On

Flying

The Art of Flexibility

The Band of Survivors

The Gift

The Perfect Switch

Through the Eyes of Grace

The Sewer

A Little Hand

What a wonderful experience to see someone you love make an eternal decision to trust in God. If you have been faithful to bring them and their need to your Heavenly Father in prayer, your great joy will be blended with an even greater sense of gratitude. How awesome that God's grace can be found with the simple move of a hand in faith.

The pastor finished his message
And then moved on to his plea,
Asking that all heads be bowed
Save his, so that he could see.

He scanned the crowd carefully
For where the Spirit might land,
When a loved one moved so slightly
And raised up a little hand.

Oh, what a day of rejoicing
At the movement of a hand,
Signaling the birth of faith,
Stepping to the Rock from sand!

We all need to see at times
The lift a little hand brings,
In the passing of daily life
And the doing of earthly things.

Helping the one who is weak,
The nursing of the aged and ill,
Assisting those whose bad choices
Have left so many needs to fill.

Whenever you lift up a hand
In assistance, in faith or in praise,
You enter a spiritual realm,
Pleasing God with your ways.

Spiritual success is accomplished
When a little hand is moved,
And the heart's desire for God
Is demonstrated and proved.

Amidst all of heaven's activity
The Savior moves to stand
"Silence please. Work to be done.
I see the raising of a little hand."

Acts 9:39-41 Then Peter arose and went with them. When he was come, they brought him into the upper chamber: and all the widows stood by him weeping, and shewing the coats and garments which Dorcas made, while she was with them. But Peter put them all forth, and kneeled down, and prayed; and turning him to the body said, Tabitha, arise. And she opened her eyes: and when she saw Peter, she sat up. And he gave her his hand, and lifted her up, and when he had called the saints and widows, presented her alive.

The Captain

Pastor Tom Downs, as a nine-year-old boy growing up in Allen Park, Michigan, knew his neighborhood well. He knew where people lived, how to get to the creek, where the pick-up games were played, and most of all whose grass was off limits. There was a fact of life that all the kids knew very well—stay off the Captain's lawn!

The Captain was not a man to be messed with or ignored. He had retired as a captain of a Great Lakes iron ore freighter and certainly was not used to having his directives disobeyed. His lawn was a cherished part of his domain and trespassing brought an immediate and severe rebuke. Any ball sailing over the fence, and into his yard, disappeared forever. Having personally experienced the Captain's verbal barrage, Tom wisely stayed clear of the forbidden turf.

At the age of ten years Tom's father instructed him to go to the Captain and volunteer to mow his lawn—for free. Tom obeyed his father and presented the offer. Since the Captain was getting on in years, he cautiously agreed to the arrangement. He then carefully instructed the young boy on his exact expectations and specifications regarding the work. Although it would later be offered, Tom was not allowed to accept payment.

Over the next several years the relationship between this youngster and the Captain grew strong. The Captain's wife made lemonade in the summer and hot chocolate in the colder months for their young helper. As time went by, Tom's lawn evangelism provided an opportunity for his father to lead this elderly couple to faith in the Lord Jesus Christ.

Tom's family moved to Taylor when he was fourteen and the days of doing the Captain's lawn were over. In a tearful farewell, the Captain thanked Tom for his years of labor and presented him with a special gift. When he retired from the ships of the Great Lakes, he had been presented him with a new captain's hat that had a special honorary gold eagle attached to the front. He gave Tom that treasured emblem that obviously meant a great deal to him. Through his faithfulness to cut the lawn, and thus invest himself in the life of this couple, Tom had obviously become much more to this man than just another neighborhood kid.

One day our labors here in this life will be over and we will stand before our Lord. If we have faithfully served Him, He will award us with a special crown of His appreciation. The thought of all He has done for us and all the blessings of eternity should make us willing to invest ourselves into the lives of others, to the best of our ability. If we do, we will see souls saved and lives blessed by God's strength working through our hands. We will also have the joy of then laying those bestowed crowns at the feet of the One who paid for our salvation with His life. Isn't God's grace a wonderful thing?!

A Message from Heaven

If a new resident in Heaven could send us a message, I wonder what would be said. Here is one possibility.

Words cannot begin to describe
The love for you I feel deep inside
For those who were so faithful,
Ones with whom I did reside.

Speech is so totally inadequate
To tell the feelings of my heart—
The joy of having been with you
Even though we're now apart.

If I had just a few more moments
I would again my devotion tell,
And say thank you one more time
Letting you know I am doing well.

Earthly language fails most of all
To describe the things I have seen.
My mouth simply cannot relay it—
Just like a heavenly dream.

My Savior is right here with me,
And those who have gone before.
Oh—all the beauty of eternity
As I stepped through the door!

I would tell you all about it—
This Heaven where I now abide,
But you must see it for yourself
Because words cannot describe.

I Corinthians 2:9 But it is written, Eye hath not seen, nor ear heard, neither have entered into the heart of man, the things which God hath prepared for them that love him.

Granny with a Red Dress On

When the oldest member of our church died this year, at the age of ninety-three, it was a story within a story. She had faithfully attended the church for many decades and was loved by the congregation. Pastor Tom called her Grandma Faye and referred to her on numerous occasions during his preaching. He had informally adopted her as a part of his personal ministry several years earlier when He started cutting her lawn. Little did he know that she would adopt him as her grandson, and capture his heart and the hearts of his entire family. Time had robbed her of many of the needed faculties of life. Her eyesight had failed (even before she quit driving) and her hearing was almost totally gone. Friends were helpful in taking her to church, to lunch, and to many places around town.

When visitors came to see her, she often wondered out loud (because of her hearing loss, out loud was really OUT LOUD) just why God had left her here in such a difficult situation. She couldn't see, she couldn't hear and even the smallest communication was very difficult. She did realize something very profound. She knew the importance of prayer and she called to her Lord on behalf of her church, her pastor, her friends and her family.

She was not shy in speaking her mind and giving Pastor Tom advice. Sometimes it came in a phone call late in the evening, which required him to mostly listen since she couldn't hear his responses. She was diligent to pray on Saturday night for Tom and the Sunday service and faithful to call on Sunday asking if anyone got saved.

Faye was a sharp dresser her whole life. She loved to wear pretty hats and was always well dressed in meticulously coordinated outfits. She even left a handwritten note pinned on a favorite red dress in her closet that said, "Bury me in this red dress, if I don't live too long"(referring to the rapture). Her wishes were followed by her family upon her death. She preached a sermon to us all on giving in the last days of her life. The last check she wrote (perhaps the last thing she wrote) was her tithe check for her church. She died just a few days later, faithful to her Lord and Savior until the very end (oops, make that the beginning).

She had planned her own funeral, right down to the songs that were sung. I believe if she could have sat up in her casket she would have preached her own funeral message. She might have concluded with "If you think I look good in this red dress, you ought see me standing next to my Savior!!"

Several months after her passing, it seems that she has spoken to us again. This message came through her executor who informed us that she had left a substantial gift to her church in her will. Apparently she managed to get the last word in, once again. Her message was, " Please use this gift to help some more people get saved." Isn't God's grace a wonderful thing?!

Flying

We are told to meditate on the things of the Lord. The solitude of an airplane flight provides a good time for this to take place. When I think of how far technology has advanced to allow us to glide safely through the air at over 30,000 feet, I am reminded of the simplicity of the gospel. At great cost on His part, He made salvation simple enough for a child to understand. What an awesome God He is!

I recently took an airplane flight—
A very smooth high flying ride,
And pondered the things of life,
From way down deep inside.

The gifts and blessings from God
Too numerous to attempt to list,
Sent from the heart of Grace,
Giving silent worship an assist.

The captain tells us all is well
As we sail above the clouds,
Over the tedious affairs of earth,
And away from airport crowds.

If this earthly captain were to
Announce something was amiss,
Then our craft began to shutter
And our engines started to miss,

I would not hope in a machine,
But in the Captain of my soul.
With His blood He paid the price
And made me spiritually whole.

What about the man next to me,
As we glide upon thin, chilly air?
Does he know and love the Savior?
Will the gospel of Christ I share?

When time starts becoming short,
And it looks like it's your turn to go,
Eternity isn't about who you are.
What's paramount is Who you know.

There is One who loves to forgive.
He covers all that's needed and then,
Death is not as much a going out—
More specifically it's a coming in.

This may seem just a little morbid
And you may be summarily right.
When taking a vacation journey,
And right in the middle of flight,

Just remember that eternal matters,
Though over the horizon, out of sight,
Must be settled in a timely manner
So you can relax and enjoy the flight.

Acts 1:8 But ye shall receive power, after that the Holy Ghost is come upon you: and ye shall be witnesses unto me both in Jerusalem, and in all Judaea, and in Samaria, and unto the uttermost part of the earth.

The Art of Flexibility

Careful, detailed plans usually insure that an event will go reasonably smooth. But sometimes things just go awry—even on that most blessed day known as the wedding day. Being a pastor with experience marrying couples in varied locations and settings, I have witnessed quite a number of humorous and even strange situations. Problems like missing rings and a misplaced license, or the difficulty of seating embittered parents who are no longer married, can usually be overcome if all involved show just a little flexibility.

I have seen attendants in the wedding party faint and have to be carried from the scene to get medical attention, with the nuptials being resumed and completed minutes later. I now jokingly tell grooms that if they pass out during the ceremony, they will wake up married, because the show must go on. In one instance, it was all I could do to contain myself as I listened to a groom accidentally distort the words to his vows as he replaced the phrase "my lawful wedded wife" with the startling phrase, "my awful leaded wife." This mistake had real meaning as the bride was a woman of considerable size. Everyone in the small, family-laden living room clearly heard the erroneous words and struggled to keep from snickering out loud.

Although many of these little problems are very memorable, none of them can compare with the story of William. He was a young man who had attended my Bible class at church for awhile. William soon found the love of his life. The new couple planned their wedding and requested that I perform the ceremony. As the wedding rehearsal day approached, an event occurred that would challenge the flexibility of us all.

William was a truck driver and on his last shift before the wedding, he pulled into his favorite truck stop for a break. After exiting his vehicle, he had an unexpected encounter with a former girl friend which did not go well and ended in his being run down by her car. His leg was broken in three places. I was called to his bedside at the hospital after surgical repairs had been completed and I talked with William and his fiancée. The idea of his leaving the hospital for a wedding the next day was medically out of the question. Postponing the wedding was not an acceptable alternative however, as many out of town guests were already on their way. With all the preparations that had been made by her family, the bride was determined to salvage as much of this—her special day—as the circumstances would allow.

Our "flexible" solution went like this. I married them in the hospital at his bedside and we recorded their vows on an audio tape. The next morning at the church the bridal party entered the church with all the precision and pomp, just as we had rehearsed. When the father of the bride walked his daughter to the front, instead of leaving he stayed with her as I informed the audience about the events of the past twenty-four hours. Although some had heard the news already, many others let out a combined gasp. The singers sang beautifully and the somewhat stunned audience listened as we played the recorded vows over the sound system. After prayer and a grand exit we all went to the church fellowship hall and enjoyed a great reception *sans* William, who remained in the hospital. I hope that someone saved him a plate of wedding food to replace the often marginal hospital fare.

Someone might wonder how this unusual wedding affected the marriage of this young couple. My answer would be that I have no idea, for I never saw or heard from them again. If they worked as hard at building their lives together as they did in the hours preceding their wedding, I am sure things have gone well.

I wonder if the "awful leaded wife" thing was actually said on purpose by that other groom. He wouldn't dare! Would he? Come to think of it, I never heard from that couple again either.

The Band of Survivors

Isn't it amazing how those who struggle against the threat of a common enemy develop such a strong camaraderie?

There is a massive army growing
With ranks that swell day by day.
No volunteers, just conscripts only—
Random selection, or so they say.

They must face a common enemy
Who has taken this land by storm,
Attacking the weak and the strong—
Certain defeat, the historical norm.

Yet today new ideas and hard work,
With a sizable dose of God's grace,
Have created this band of survivors,
Who ran with cancer, and won the race.

In their victory, your support was vital.
Now they're asking you to help again.
Together attacking this deadly enemy
So others who are threatened can win.

Dedicated to cancer survivors everywhere, and their ongoing fight to find a cure for this deadly disease. For information on how you can help, contact The American Cancer Society.

The Gift

It was our 5th annual Christmas party for needy families and the gymnasium was packed. Seventy families from our church had each adopted one of these families and purchased gifts for them with special emphasis on the children. There was food, music, games and even one of those bouncy, air-inflated, moon-walk things on the balcony.

Inside the locker rooms were bags of gifts, numbered for each family involved in the program. Sometimes unexpected families would arrive who were not on the official list. Amos, the director of the project, had planned for this contingency by arranging for extra "just-in-case" gifts to be donated. When unregistered families arrived, we scrambled and put together a gift assortment that met their particular needs.

Just prior to the presentation of the gifts, our pastor had everyone stop their activities while he told them the story about God's special gift of His Son. About a dozen adults and numerous children raised their hands indicating that they had prayed with Pastor Tom and invited Jesus into their lives as their Lord and Savior. That was a wonderful blessing, but the night was not over.

The signal was given and the bags of gifts were delivered to their intended families. The sounds of tearing paper and squeals of glee filled the gym. One of the volunteers informed Amos that an 11 year old girl had unexpectedly come with a family as a guest and when everything had been passed out it was realized that she had not received a gift. After checking he found that every spare gift had been needed and was previously distributed. The extra gift cupboard was completely empty. Amos told the volunteers that there was nothing we could do to get her a gift at that late hour.

The idea that she was having a good time with the food and the activities of the evening would have to do for the time being. We would all have to trust that God was at work in all the details, even when it seemed that things were not coming out right.

At about that same time our pastor was circulating through the crowd enjoying that tremendous scene, when this same little 11 year old girl tugged at his sleeve. “Would you say that again?” she asked him. “Say what, Honey?” he replied. “Would you tell me again about how the baby Jesus was God’s special gift?” Pastor Tom had the privilege of sitting at a table with her and telling her again the story of God’s great love for her. Within a few minutes she bowed her head and asked God for the gift of Jesus in her life. With tears in her eyes she told our pastor, whose tears were also freely flowing, that she had gotten the best gift ever this Christmas. She had gotten Jesus.

Concerned people were troubled that there was no gift left for this child that night, but sometimes we just don’t see the big picture. We had done our best, but just didn’t have a gift for her. At that very moment, in another area of the gym, God moved in and provided several special gifts for her. He gave her Jesus, the Holy Spirit, a new heart, and eternal life. Isn’t God’s grace a wonderful thing?

The Perfect Switch

A friend of mine, J. S. Thomas, told me about growing up in Ewing Virginia as a member of a family with thirteen children. His father worked on the railroad and would often be gone from home two days at a time. When it came to discipline, all accounts would be settled upon his return home. This did not preclude his mother from taking care of this area of their childhood education, if the situation warranted it.

His brother Johnnie often began winding up the day Dad left and would soon be pushing the willingness of his mom to withhold physical punishment until her husband's return. Although he was often guilty of provoking his brother to higher levels of foolishness, he usually knew when to duck and take a low profile.

There was one particular time when his Mom had endured quite enough of his brother's antics, she directed J. S. to go and harvest a switch for her to use on Johnnie. He was more than willing to be of service. The fact of the matter was that he was delighted to be of help. You see, this could not be just any old switch, he decided, it must be a great one. "My brother deserves nothing but the best," he chortled.

He cut one branch after another and gleefully tested them and chose the one that appeared most durable. As he trimmed the small shoots from the switch he was careful to leave small nubbins in place. They would add to the effectiveness of the switch, he surmised. He felt that he held in his hand, the perfect switch.

Feeling that he had done his best to see to it that Johnnie got what he deserved, he returned and presented this masterpiece to his mother. She looked at his work and looked again at him and said,

"J. S., you have been pretty ornery also. I better just whip you too." Which she promptly proceeded to do.

That day he learned the practical truth of Proverbs 24:17, "Rejoice not when thy enemy falleth, and let not thine heart be glad when he stumbleth:" If only he had shown a little compassion with his brother, life would have gone a lot better for him that day. Perhaps there is a lesson here for us all.

Through the eyes of Grace

How quickly we jump to conclusions about someone's actions or attitudes and become judgmental. Since God has so graciously forgiven us of every sin through His Son Jesus Christ, it seems that our gratitude should be demonstrated in our reactions to others. As forgiven sinners, we ought to be people who are eager and ready to forgive the failures of others. Getting bent out of shape at the smallest offense will not be a characteristic of one who has abundantly received God's mercy and grace.

The Father was looking down one day
At all of us in the human race.
His view was one of compassion,
Looking through the eyes of grace.

"I will send them My salvation.
It will be packaged within My Son.
His death will pay for their sin.
For a Savior, He's the only one.

Hereafter My view is optional,
Whether as a judge or a father,
Forgiving all those who will call,
Condemning all who don't bother."

When Jesus has entered the picture
And every bit of sin does erase,
God watches my life continually
With only the eyes of Grace.

I am not even close to perfect.
He of all knows that very fact

And patiently and firmly corrects
Each and every rebellious act.

Now where is this story going
And what is there here to learn?
That God looks at my actions,
Shows me something to discern.

His kindness in my weakness
Is offered to a repentant heart.
With the grace of understanding
I receive a brand new start.

As I consider the lives of others
And the stress upon each face,
Surely I must view my brother,
Looking through the eyes of grace.

John 8:4-9 They say unto him, Master, this woman was taken in adultery, in the very act. Now Moses in the law commanded us, that such should be stoned: but what sayest thou? his they said, tempting him, that they might have to accuse him. But Jesus stooped down, and with his finger wrote on the ground, as though he heard them not. So when they continued asking him, he lifted up himself, and said unto them, He that is without sin among you, let him first cast a stone at her. And again he stooped down, and wrote on the ground. And they which heard it, being convicted by their own conscience, went out one by one, beginning at the eldest, even unto the last: and Jesus was left alone, and the woman standing in the midst.

The Sewer

I'm not only the administrator of a Christian school but also the instructor of a ninth grade Bible class. Each year my class looks forward to the "Sewer Story" from my junior high days. It is always good for them to understand that their authorities were teenagers once and lived through some very unusual things.

One winter in Detroit, Michigan, a group of my young friends and I discovered the tunnels on the Rouge River. These were large concrete storm drains that extended back into the bank of the river. We accessed them by walking out on the frozen river into these five foot cylinders filled with darkness. These were parallel tunnels that merged together after a lengthy walk in darkness so thick that if the flashlights we carried were extinguished, you wouldn't be able to see your hand in front of your face. The unified tunnel continued back into the ground quite far, ending at what we called "the underground stream." This was a trough of water that flowed back into a small opening to who knows where. If you were looking down on the tunnel configuration from above, it would look like a capital letter Y.

We enjoyed exploring what we called "the caves" and realized that from the deepest part, we could turn off the flashlights and exit the tunnel safely by placing our fingers along the wall while jogging back toward the river. After some distance of pitch black, we would begin to faintly see the light up ahead signaling the entrance. It was after one of these dark exits that the idea came to us.

Since we knew the secret of how to exit, we decided we would share some of this excitement and suspense with a few of our "closest friends." So we recruited one or two of them to join us in exploring "the caves." We instructed them to dress warm, wear boots, and we would bring everything else needed for this great adventure. After taking them to the back of the tunnel using our flashlights, we turned the lights off, plunging ourselves into total darkness. Of course we knew the way to exit and pressing our fingers against the wall, we ran out, screaming, leaving our guests stranded, alone in the tunnel in the dark.

Some may interpret these actions as cruel and insensitive, but remember, as the explorers felt their way along, they were always headed out, no matter which tunnel they chose at the junction. We waited at the entrance and tried our best to holler the scariest noises we could think up. Without fail they would soon emerge, quite scared, shaken, and seriously considering doing us great bodily harm. After they had some time to settle down, we showed them how the tunnels were configured and that they were never truly in danger at any time. Now what do you think their next thought was after realizing what had occurred to them? That's right--- they immediately began to think of some "close friends" who would enjoy a good thrill. These friends would become the next victims of this delightful scam. Why is it that a good trick is always more fun when it is played on someone else?

Invariably one of my students will ask what my parents thought of our exploring adventures and general meanness. My answer--- Mom and Dad never found out, but God knew all about it and the nature of my heart and that I needed a true relationship with Him through His Son. I thank God that by His grace that kid from the sewers grew up to become a minister and Christian school administrator who now enjoys teaching kids to show kindness to one another.

I find it amazing though, how surprised we parents sometimes act when our teenagers do some really stupid and dangerous things. Before we react too strongly it would be advisable for us to remember some of the foolish escapades of our youth. While we live in a more dangerous world now and careful limits must be put in place to insure the safety of our young people, remember that when you ask a youth why he did a stupid thing, and he answers, "I don't know," he may very well be telling you the truth.

Music

An Instrument of Grace

Come and Whisper

The Concert of Grace

The Song of Grace

The Symphony

When He Reached Down His Hand

An Instrument of Grace

I remember being impressed by a poem I first heard many years ago entitled "The Touch of the Master's Hand" by Myra Brooks Welch. It was a story about an old violin that was considered worthless, at an auction, until a master violinist picked it up and played it beautifully. It is so important that we who have felt the restoring touch of God's love in our lives remain usable by allowing Him to tune us daily. Left on my own, I seem to specialize in sour notes, but in His care and with His touch I am a part of the symphony of grace.

Lord, help me be an instrument
Within Your orchestra of grace,
Played by the Maestro of Mercy
At the perfect rhythm and pace.

The song of the redeemed
Played from first tenor to bass,
With the harmony of Heaven—
The great symphony of grace.

I pray that You will tune me
As we share a time each day,
That I won't produce discord
In anything I do and say.

Help me focus on Your hand
As You lead my heart along
Let the notes of my life resound
Like a heavenly praise song.

And as I look back on my life
When Your eternity I embrace

I will praise You for making me
An instrument of grace

Ezekiel 33:32 And, lo, thou art unto them as a very lovely song of one that hath a pleasant voice, and can play well on an instrument:…

Come and Whisper

Many times the noise of living prevents us from hearing the voice of God. The prophet Elijah had to stop and listen for the still small voice of God, and we must also. Don't get too busy to pause and let God whisper to your heart.

When the quake moves the ground
And life's storms are all around
Let the focus of my heart be found
On a whisper from Your heart.

When the storm passes through
And I forget to look for You
Bid me come, my course renew
In the whisper from Your heart.

Let me linger ever near
For words my heart must hear
Pushing past the outward ear
To the spirit deep within.

Come and whisper to my heart
That from sin I may depart
Lord I need a brand new start
Come whisper, whisper to my heart.

1 Kings 19:11-13 And he said, Go forth, and stand upon the mount before the LORD. And, behold, the LORD passed by, and a great and strong wind rent the mountains, and brake in pieces the rocks before the LORD; but the LORD was not in the wind: and after the wind an earthquake; but the LORD was not in the earthquake: And after the earthquake a fire; but the LORD was not in the fire: and after the fire a still small voice.

The Concert of Grace

The more I think about that great heavenly scene when we are around God's throne, the more I realize the limitations of my finite mind. God has told us, in His word, that our imaginations are not capable of accurately comprehending all that He has prepared for us. It is enjoyable, however, to ponder about how things might be on that great day.

If I were writing a song
Entitled the *Song of Grace*
To be sung around the throne
As we stand before His face,

What stanzas would I include?
What things would I want to say,
In expressing my admiration,
Placing my attitude on display?

"Hallelujah—what a Savior!"
Would begin this graceful song.
"He suffered to buy our pardon,"
Would echo from the throng.

"Worthy, oh so very worthy,
This perfect Lamb that was slain
To purchase our redemption
And then rose to live again.

"Forgiven, yes totally forgiven,
Washed much whiter than snow,
Cleansed by Calvary's sacrifice
When the Savior's blood did flow."

This great heavenly song
Many questions would frame

Like, why would He love me so
Since I vainly used His name?

Amazed we stand in great awe
Of He Who wrote the great plan
Before the creation of the world
To redeem each willing man.

This wonderful worship anthem
Comprised of voices redeemed—
In an ultimate perfect harmony
Rejoicing as they had dreamed.

I started out singing first tenor
As the verses began to unfold.
Then I moved to the base section
And sang those notes so bold.

We sang of God's great mercy
The wonderful gift of His love
That called us to Mt. Calvary
And then to our home above.

Oh what a wonderful Savior
Who has been a friend so dear!
Someday we will stand singing
In His glorious presence so near.

Now, if you have never met Him
Make your heart His special place,
Then join with this heavenly choir
In singing the *Song of Grace.*

Revelation 5:9 And they sung a new song, saying, Thou art worthy to take the book, and to open the seals thereof: for thou wast slain, and hast redeemed us to God by thy blood out of every kindred, and tongue, and people, and nation;

The Song of Grace

Singing hymns and spiritual songs does not guarantee us a worshipping experience. All too often singing is done in a manner that engages the memory, but not the spirit. Even worship leaders can allow their singing to become a mechanical performance. However, when the leaders present to us songs that have been written on a spiritual level, and we engage our hearts as well as our minds, worship is a wonderful result.

Singers come and singers go.
Songs have filled this place,
Beautiful notes and rhythms,
Touching and stirring the faith.

Some songs present a story of
The soul that's been set free,
Escaping the bondage of sin
And its eternal death decree.

There are other songs of praise
That lift our spirits up on high
And thank our heavenly Father
For His Son Who came to die.

Writers seek for special words
To make their songs unique,
And relate a spiritual truth
That to our hearts will speak.

There is a required ingredient
For a song that touches the heart:
We must experience first hand
The message it seeks to impart.

If those who minister in song
Have welcomed God's embrace,
Thus cleansed they can deliver
A thing called the song of grace.

Words that will share the truth
And draw sincere listeners in,
With simple notes and phrases
Causing true worship to begin.

God has given such a message
That transforms and sanctifies
And provides the heart a voice
While enlightening blinded eyes.

So listen very carefully when
Musicians have sought His face.
Then join with them in singing
The wonderful song of grace.

Colossians 3:16 Let the word of Christ dwell in you richly in all wisdom; teaching and admonishing one another in psalms and hymns and spiritual songs, singing with grace in your hearts to the Lord.

The Symphony

I was sitting in the Detroit Symphony Hall, anticipating a program designed to introduce the symphony to students from area schools. Our group was escorted to seats that were right in front of the orchestra. I had been hoping for good seats since we were to be seated by schools, in whatever way the ushers directed, and I was not disappointed.

As we waited for the performance to begin, I noticed the musicians entering the stage and warming up, each with his particular instrument. I could see the string section best since they were located closest to where we were seated. As I watched, I realized that they were not just warming up, but they were actually tuning their instruments. These professionals, with valuable and time-tested musical instruments were carefully checking the sound that was being produced. They then made the needed adjustments that would allow the production of just the right tones. These musicians apparently fully understood that an instrument that was not properly tuned was of little use to the orchestra and its conductor as they attempted to present a quality reproduction of the composer's work. Each member of the orchestra shares a responsibility to be in harmony by being properly tuned.

I began to consider spiritual things and the idea that God desires to produce a great harmony of grace by using our lives as instruments. It is imperative that we develop our skills and grow in our spiritual abilities as the great musicians sitting before me had developed their musical skills. Yet if we do not take time for a spiritual tune-up, the results will be disharmony. Our sound will be off key and the symphony of grace will be harmed.

As educational professionals, we need to be diligent to tune-up our academic skills in order to produce the desired results in the lives of our students. We also need to be strong and under control in our spirit so that we may be the role models that young people so desperately need today.

A spiritual tune-up occurs during our time alone with God and His word. Do you want to be a blessing to the audience that watches your life? Tune-up on a regular basis and then play with the harmony and passion of a heart that is fully usable in the Master's hand.

When He Reached Down His Hand for Me

In the spring of 1973, double bypass heart surgery had been performed on A. T. Humphries, but his future certainly did not look bright. He actually hung between life and death for forty days. The endotracheal tube that had been a part of the wonderful medical equipment that had kept him alive had also damaged his vocal cords. Music ministry had been the focus of his life. He had been a minister of music, a college music professor, and a music evangelist, and now that wonderful part of his life was probably gone forever. In his despair, he wondered if it would not have been the best thing to have died and gone to be with the Lord. He questioned why God had not reached down and just taken him home. God was reaching down, but not in the manner that A. T. was pondering.

In spite of hospital rules about the age of visitors, his wife Bobbie brought his children to visit their father. His prognosis had been very guarded, and with no assurances of his survival she was determined to let them see him. It was during one of these visits that his 2 ½ year old son Amos patted his father's stomach and said, "I wuv you daddy." With the words of that little child, a deeply spiritual work began in the heart of this gravely ill man.

In his younger and healthier days he had served the Lord with his talent and strength, but now both were gone with his broken voice and weakened body. Realizing the important and yet incomplete work of raising his family, he asked the Lord to allow him to live long enough to see his young son grow up to be a man. That would require him to function for almost twenty years with a damaged heart. The remaining days of his life were surrendered to serve a sovereign God within the limitations of his physical weakness.

One year after his heart surgery, he still could barely speak above a whisper. He had a throat specialist re-examine his damaged voice. The doctor told him that there was nothing more that could be done and that in his opinion, the damage was permanent. As A. T. drove from that appointment he began worshiping the Lord by humming and then suddenly sang *Amazing Grace* in full voice. He was thrilled, but puzzled about what God was doing in his life.

That summer A. T. returned to his beloved music on a limited basis. His voice was not what it used to be, but God was blessing his life and ministry. He had been a dear friend of my grandfather for many years, but it was not until this time in his life that I realized who he was and became aware of what a wonderful history he had in musical ministry.

We had started Baptist Park Christian School in 1974 and God was blessing us with many students thus requiring additions to our teaching staff. In the summer of 1975 I realized that as the school administrator it would be necessary for me to leave Michigan and visit college campuses in search of teachers. In the fall I attended a conference at Liberty Baptist College in Lynchburg, Virginia, with a twofold purpose in mind. I wanted to see what God was doing there so I could confidently recommend this school to my students and I also wanted to know if I could recruit quality teacher candidates in the future. Little did I know that three of my own children would one day be blessed by and graduate from Liberty University, on a Liberty mountain campus that did not even exist in 1975.

I certainly did not really expect to see anyone I knew at the conference, least of all A. T. Humphries. He had come to the conference to see first hand a ministry that his old friend, evangelist B. R. Lakin, had mentioned to him on several occasions. A. T. had ministered with Dr. Lakin in numerous evangelistic meetings over many years. When he arrived in Lynchburg he registered at the hotel where Dr. Lakin was staying and was soon introduced to Dr. Jerry Falwell. The two of them seemed to hit it off right from the first moment they met.

Dr. Falwell asked A. T. to sing at the conference and that is where I come back into the story. I was walking into the Thomas Road Baptist Church for the evening service and in front of me stood A. T. Humphries. He told me that Jerry had asked him to sing that night and was glad that someone from Gilead was in attendance.

I found a seat two rows behind the center aisle and waited for the service to begin. I watched as young talents Robbie Hiner, Mac Evans and, I believe, Kendra Cook, sang in the earlier portion of the service. I began to pray for A. T. because I knew his voice tone for tone could not match up with the vocalists who had preceded him. His widow, Bobbie Humphries, told me that A. T. was worried as well.

Finally it was his turn to sing and when he did, he introduced Dr. Falwell and all in attendance, to a song that would become the most recognized theme of the rest of his life. The song was *When He Reached Down His Hand for Me.* That song worked powerfully in my heart and I watched with tears in my eyes as the preachers in that audience got fired up. It seems that we could all identify with the line "I was lost and undone, without God and His Son, when He reached down His hand for me." Preachers began to shout and some stood up and slapped their Bibles over their heads. Even as God was reminding me of the pit He pulled me out of, I couldn't help wondering what many Baptist congregations across the country would think if they saw their preacher so physically involved in a worship session. I believe we have come a long way since then in our freedom to worship with enthusiasm.

When A. T. Humphries had come out of that hospital alive several years earlier he had made a special commitment to God. He gave Him all that he had left and God blessed his weakness with grace. Dr. Humphries was able to use those damaged vocal cords to minister to more hearts in his latter years as he traveled across the entire country, than in all of his previous years of service combined. God also allowed his wounded heart to beat long enough to see his son reach his senior year at Liberty University.

Today God is still seeking people who will give Him all that they are and all the time they have left. When they make that commitment like A. T. Humphries did, God's strength is perfected in their weakness. God will reach down and bless your life beyond your highest expectations. I was privileged to see it happen with my own eyes in the life of my friend, Dr. A. T. Humphries. Isn't God's grace a wonderful thing?!

Bible Themes

Come and See

My Crowns

No Room

The Borders of Obedience

The Crown Jewel

Currents of Grace

The Harlot

The Passion

The Path to the Resurrection

To Win a Child

Sandals of Grace

The Shadow of Grace

Come and See

Our first night at Kids' Kamp was going well when the gospel was explained and kids were invited to go and talk to someone about asking Jesus to forgive their sins. Many children responded and headed back to a designated place where counselors were waiting for them. My responsibility was to facilitate the process by seeing that all the children had someone to talk to them.

One little seven-year-old girl sat with one of our ladies who carefully explained to her how she could become God's child by asking Jesus to come into her life and forgive her of all of her sins. This little girl soaked up every word, soon prayed a simple prayer of faith, and was thrilled afterward.

If that was the end of the story, it would be a wonderful account of God saving the soul of a child. The story did not end there. The girl proceeded to ask the counselor if she would wait at their meeting place for a minute while she went to get her nine-year-old brother who was still in the auditorium. She soon located him and brought him back with her. He wondered what it was that she wanted him to hear. She led him to her counselor so he could listen to her story. He listened and he too trusted in Jesus to forgive him and come live in his heart.

As I watched those events unfold, I was reminded of the story in the Bible, where Andrew met Jesus and then went and got his brother Simon Peter and brought him to the Lord. I remembered later that Phillip had done the very same thing when he found Nathaniel and brought him to Jesus.

A little seven-year-old girl has demonstrated to us all an action that God loves to see in our lives. Remember the joy and freedom that came in the early days of your relationship with the Savior? Do you recall that intense desire that you had to invite others to come and experience the Lord?

Jesus continues to call a lost and dying world to come to Himself, that He might give them a new life. He is still looking for Christians who will invite those that are around them to "come and see". If you will be faithful to simply invite others to the Savior, God will take care of everything else. Isn't God's grace a wonderful thing?!

John 1:43-46 The day following Jesus would go forth into Galilee, and findeth Philip, and saith unto him, Follow me. Now Philip was of Bethsaida, the city of Andrew and Peter. Philip findeth Nathanael, and saith unto him, we have found him, of whom Moses in the law, and the prophets, did write, Jesus of Nazareth, the son of Joseph. And Nathanael said unto him, can there any good thing come out of Nazareth? Philip saith unto him, Come and see.

My Crowns

I was thinking recently about the blessing it has been to my heart to become the grandfather of six children. The idea of enjoying them and then being able to give them back to Mom and Dad when they get fussy is very appealing. However, as my love for them began to grow, my spirit became burdened about their future. I understand that parents are the first in line to teach their children, but that does not excuse me from being involved. I also realize that I have a great responsibility and privilege to help teach them about the things of God. My grandparents taught me many things about the Lord that I will never forget. I desire for my grandchildren that they grow up in grace, thanking God that He gave them a heritage of those who fear His name. Leave your family an inheritance of true riches, one of eternal spiritual treasures.

The Bible calls grandchildren
The crowns of an old man,
Though until just recently
I didn't really understand.

Wondering if it would happen
As my life kept moving along,
The mystery remained unsolved
As the desire was getting strong.

Finally the good news came!
All conditions had been met.
Patience would still be needed.
Joy on the way, but not yet.

How wonderful is their coming!
With great fanfare they arrive.
Once the painful dues are paid,
Now so animated and fully alive.

We try our very best to decipher
Just whom they favor the most.
Remembering to thank the Giver—
Father, Son, and Holy Ghost.

Now that my crowns are here
I begin to realize a great truth.
The pleasure they bring to my heart
Couldn't be experienced in youth.

Now I must do my part, Lord,
To show them the wisdom of age.
The things You have taught to me
In the passing of each living phase.

These crowns are very precious.
They must be kept safe and secure.
Jesus, I'll leave them in Your care,
A faithful guardian, to be sure.

Proverbs: 17:6 Children's children are the crown of old men; and the glory of children are their fathers.

Psalm: 61:5 For thou, O God, hast heard my vows; thou hast given me the heritage of those who fear thy name.

No Room

When I read again about the birth of our Savior, I am reminded afresh how my life parallels some of the circumstances. I wonder how often I personally have hung out the—no vacancy—sign in my heart, just like the innkeeper of that day in Bethlehem.

No room in that Bethlehem inn
The coming Christ child would find.
No room for this burdened family—
Out of sight and also out of mind.

Let them stay outside—out back,
Where the animals and livestock lay.
No place here for the weary to rest;
They will just have to settle for hay.

Things haven't changed that much
In the manner of our living today.
As the pace of life has quickened
Still "No room" is what many say.

"No Vacancy" flashes out brightly.
It seems our lives are just too full
Of the important issues and items,
With busy details a constant pull.

Some have no room for the Savior
And His Calvary sacrifice so dear.
A careless, eternal, uncertainty
With His return predictably near.

Other hearts invited His entrance
Putting eternal guarantees in place,

Yet an old sign has now re-emerged
"No Vacancy"—no available space.

His word has offered its touch,
The response—"Still no room."
With marriages, families and jobs,
Constant activities always loom.

Do you have room for the Master
In your heart, your life, your mind?
The Spirit and His word are knocking.
Will a permanent lodging they find?

Luke 2:7 And she brought forth her firstborn son, and wrapped him in swaddling clothes, and laid him in a manger; because there was no room for them in the inn.

The Borders of Obedience

For the Christian, success in life is directly tied to the level of our obedience to God's word. This is a simple precept that we too often make difficult with bad choices.

I remember the rules of childhood
And the things to be done each day,
All the limitations that were given
For me to adhere to along my way.

Authorities expected obedience,
A complete effort on my part,
To live by specific guidelines
Performing them from the heart.

They often desired more of me
Than I was really willing to yield,
At times accepting partial success
Whenever I passionately appealed.

It provided them a sense of control
When the limits were set in place
Avoidance of direct confrontation
While giving the subordinate space.

The Lord Jesus is now my Master.
With a specific plan for my life
He knows all the hidden pitfalls
And the temptations that are rife.

He is a determined Taskmaster,
One who desires to see me grow.
But to Him my partial obedience
Is synonymous with saying, 'no.'

So I'll pray the prayer of Jabez
And apply it to my sinful heart.
"Expand my borders of obedience
Because I've only given You part.

"Enlarge my ability, dear Father,
To say, 'yes,' to You every day,
And seek to humbly serve You
By being ready always to obey.

"This request sounds contradictory
Coming from someone so intense
In the pursuit and desire to have
My own way at others' expense.

"Please Father, You know me best,
I have sat too long on the fence.
Help me reach to new distances
In the borders of my obedience."

When the adjustments are made,
And my faithfulness has grown,
The praise, the glory, the honor
Simply could never be my own.

May the blessings that others see
From the response I have desired,
Encourage them to imitate Jabez
By whose prayer I was inspired.

I Chron. 4:9&10 And Jabez was more honourable than his brethren: and his mother called his name Jabez, saying, Because I bare him with sorrow. And Jabez called on the God of Israel, saying, Oh that thou wouldest bless me indeed, and enlarge my coast, and that thine hand might be with me, and that thou wouldest keep me from evil, that it may not grieve me! And God granted him that which he requested.

The Crown Jewel

On a trip to London, England, I visited the Tower of London and view the Crown Jewels. I remember looking at a beautiful crown and the fantastic jewel that was at the center of the royal diadem. There will be many beautiful things in Heaven, but none more precious than our Lord Jesus Christ. Just wait until we see Him.

Grace is a wonderful thing
When it is worn like a crown
Changing who we really are
From our head right on down.

Bestowed upon the unworthy
As a token of His great love—
Its price beyond all measure,
And its origin Heaven above.

This precious graceful crown
Has a jewel that is set in place
Tempered in sorrow at Calvary
He is the Crown Jewel of Grace.

When viewed by fleshly eyes
The value cannot be perceived,
For it only becomes a treasure
When by faith it is received.

This wonderful heavenly jewel!
Jesus Christ is His given name,
The centerpiece of all creation,
Salvation is the reason He came.

Reset after His resurrection,
He bedecks His Father's throne,
Patiently waiting with open arms,
To welcome His children home.

His atonement provides the way
And His hands prepare a place.
He will rule there forevermore
As the Crown Jewel of Grace.

Hebrews 2:9 But we see Jesus, who was made a little lower than the angels for the suffering of death, crowned with glory and honor; that he by the grace of God should taste death for every man.

Currents of Grace

I cannot imagine a more desperate situation, in life, then Moses' mother faced that day in Egypt. She gave her child to God's grace and was blessed beyond measure. As a parent, I understand that totally trusting God with your most treasured possession is easier said than done.

What a desperate life circumstance
For a young Jewish mother to endure,
Unable to protect the life of her son,
No available safe choices, to be sure.

He was born into a time of adversity,
A very unsettled and dangerous place,
Secretly cradled in a basket of faith,
Launched out in the currents of grace.

God used her trusting faith that day
To put her son in the palace of a king,
Thus inaugurating a course of events
That freedom to a nation would bring.

She couldn't have known the outcome
As she lovingly weaved that little ark,
Motivated by a mother's love and faith
When the future looked hopelessly dark.

Yet it was on a fearful and fateful day
With her abiding trust of God in place,
She released her beloved child aboard
An ark of faith on the currents of grace.

She didn't survive long enough to see
The development and end of the story
In the miraculous life of that infant son—
The way he would give God the glory.

God is still calling on mothers today
As dangerous waters around us flow,
"Give Me what time won't let you keep.
Watch My grace work when you let go."

Exodus 2:3 And when she could not longer hide him, she took for him an ark of bulrushes, and daubed it with slime and with pitch, and put the child therein; and she laid it in the flags by the river's brink.

The Harlot

Joshua tells us a story about a woman who lived in one of the saddest lifestyles I can imagine. She sold herself to sin on a daily basis. Yet as I think about it I realize that I sometimes do the same thing, only with sins that I consider nicer than hers. In either situation, the grace of God is needed to turn defeat into victory.

She had heard about their coming,
And great miracles along the way.
Her heart was troubled and moved,
To just what end she couldn't say.

Life had become a sad confusion
Of many emotions lost in sorrow.
As she sold her soul in small pieces,
There was little left for tomorrow.

Hopefully there was more to live for
Than the grisly regimen of her sin.
Perhaps in this new confrontation
Her heart could be renewed again.

Would she help hide these strangers
Who had come to spy out the land?
The hope of redemption now dawned.
With God she would make her stand.

She trembled as the events unfolded,
Her life and her family on the line.
The men escaped to give their report,
But not before teaching her the sign.

"Gather your family inside the door.
Hang a scarlet thread from the sill.
When judgment comes to your world,
This house will be standing still."

Her simple faith was noted by God
When His army executed the plan.
Jericho fell in pieces to the ground—
Except Rahab and all of her clan.

She ended up forgiven and cleansed
From all the sins that filled her world,
And God's scarlet thread connected her
To a wonderful future as yet unfurled.

A harlot, by grace, became a matriarch
In the line of King David and our Lord.
Remembered for faithfulness forever,
Eternal righteousness was her reward.

Do you have a problem with sin that
Is making life's horizon look bleak?
Have you sold your heart to the world
Through the treasures that you seek?

Take hold of God's scarlet thread.
It represents the Savior's shed blood,
That cleanses us whiter than snow,
From sins that pour in like a flood.

Feel His great hand cover your life
When the storms of judgment blow.
Watch while your future expands,
And by His grace you begin to grow.

Joshua 6:25 And Joshua saved Rahab the harlot alive, and her father's household, and all that she had; and she dwelleth in Israel even unto this day; because she hid the messengers, which Joshua sent to spy out Jericho.

Hebrews 11:31 By faith the harlot Rahab perished not with them that believed not, when she had received the spies with peace

The Passion

I believe that in these last days God has put His Son on display in a most dramatic fashion for the whole world to see. This graphic portrayal has shaken many Christians to their very foundations with feelings of personal responsibility for the suffering of Jesus Christ. Those who witness this display, having never come to terms with the Lord, will undoubtedly be challenged to seriously consider the Biblical call to salvation through the sacrifice of the Savior.

Disturbing, so truly disturbing
As I watched that giant screen,
Witnessing the suffering of Jesus
In a way I'd not previously seen.

That cruel and vicious scourging,
A horror I now better understand,
As strokes were laid upon Him,
Seems the whip was in my hand.

It was for me that He suffered
The thorns piercing to the bone,
Crowned with briars grown wild
From rebellious seeds I'd sown.

Nails driven into hands and feet
From a hammer swinging true,
That pinned Him to a cruel tree
To die there, in full public view.

The mocking, hitting, and spitting—
Our Lord and Savior, He bore it all.
Then even when I turned my back
My hard heart still heard His call.

Thank You for paying that price!
It is by Your death I was set free.
And yet I will never understand
What your love ever saw in me.

One day I will stand before You.
Then face-to-face we will meet.
Honored—I'll call You Worthy—
Laying my crowns at Your feet.

Isaiah 53:3-6 He is despised and rejected of men; a man of sorrows, and acquainted with grief: and we hid as it were our faces from him; he was despised, and we esteemed him not. Surely he hath borne our griefs, and carried our sorrows: yet we did esteem him stricken, smitten of God, and afflicted. But he was wounded for our transgressions, he was bruised for our iniquities: the chastisement of our peace was upon him; and with his stripes we are healed. All we like sheep have gone astray; we have turned every one to his own way; and the LORD hath laid on him the iniquity of us all.

The Path to the Resurrection

Our rejoicing on Easter Sunday over the resurrection of Jesus Christ must never eclipse the remembering of the terrible price that was paid at Calvary. When we take our hearts on a solemn journey through the events of Friday, the celebration of His Sunday resurrection is flooded with the joy of a finished redemption.

Oh how we love Easter Sunday!
When Jesus came out of the grave
Completing the spiritual redemption
Of the fallen race He came to save.

Joy had swept through the ranks
Of those who loved Him so dear.
Their next dinner was very special
With the risen Jesus sitting near.

Rejoicing is an important process,
Although we must not fail to see
That the path to the resurrection
Leads directly through Calvary.

A plan authored before creation
To deal with the entrance of sin,
Allowing all men to be redeemed
Who, through faith, are born again.

Celebrate on Easter Sunday morning,
For by grace we have been set free!
But never forget the price He paid
That Passover Friday at Calvary.

Isaiah 53:4-6 Surely he hath borne our griefs, and carried our sorrows: yet we did esteem him stricken, smitten of God, and afflicted. But he was wounded for our transgressions, he was bruised for our iniquities: the chastisement of our peace was upon him; and with his stripes we are healed. All we like sheep have gone astray; we have turned every one to his own way; and the LORD hath laid on him the iniquity of us all.

To Win a Child

I've had the privilege of leading children to Christ and watching as others have led children to the Lord. It is a wonderful blessing to listen to the simple prayer of a child. It is also important to reach them at a tender age before years of wrong choices make their life decisions much more difficult.

Sing them a love song about Jesus,
One that tells all about His grace,
The freedom His presence brings,
And mercy's breeze upon the face.

Read to them about God's Son—
The amazing details about His life,
The day He climbed up Calvary
To become that perfect sacrifice.

Teach them words from the Bible
That create a new life on the inside,
And the goodness of God's love
When in Him they choose to abide.

Tell them your personal experience
About what God has done for you—
All of the blessings and good times,
His faithfulness in tough times, too.

Show them a commitment to God—
One that practices the faithful walk,
By displaying a life that is genuine
With right actions and not just talk.

Sing to them, read, teach and tell—
Stories of God the Father and Son,
And when the Spirit speaks to them,
Into His loving arms they will run.

Mark 10:13-15 And they brought young children to him, that he should touch them: and his disciples rebuked those that brought them. But when Jesus saw it, he was much displeased, and said unto them, Suffer the little children to come unto me, and forbid them not: for of such is the kingdom of God. Verily I say unto you, Whosoever shall not receive the kingdom of God as a little child, he shall not enter therein.

Sandals of Grace

Do you suppose that a repentant son would ever forget the day his father put sandals of grace upon feet that had been damaged by sin? I know I will never forget, how about you?

I remember so very well the events
Of that prideful and arrogant day,
When I chose to do my own thing
And from my Father—walk away.

I wore the ring of my inheritance
And the coat of blessing as well,
As I journeyed out into the world
In its corruption decided to dwell.

I remember the day they were gone—
The parties, the friends, the crowd
When my funds had been exhausted,
The silence became incredibly loud.

I had traded provided sandals of grace
For the blistered soles of rebellion,
And exchanged my coat of blessing
For rags of a common street hellion.

The precious ring of my inheritance
Was for my immediate survival sold,
As I pawned it for a worthless supply
Of this world's deceptive fool's gold.

I remember the day my heart decided
To travel rebellion's road in reverse.

I had not accomplished much as a son—
My a track record of life even worse.

My Father ran to me as I crested the hill,
With forgiveness and love in His heart.
He offered again the things I had traded
And gave this humbled son a new start.

I remember that special day most of all
When He put sandals on repenting feet,
That had conveyed me back to the place
Where my God's grace and mercy meet.

Luke 15:22-24 "But the father said to his servants, "Bring out the best robe and put it on him, and put a ring on his hand and sandals on his feet. And bring the fatted calf here and kill it, and let us eat and be merry; for this my son was dead and is alive again; he was lost and is found.' And they began to be merry.

The Shadow of Grace

A friend of mine wrote a song entitled *The Shadow of the Cross* that I particularly enjoyed singing. As I thought about the grace of God that covers us, I couldn't help but wonder about the type of a shadow that grace might cast. Here is one possibility.

The steps of life have been many
With ups and downs along the way,
My directions not always the best,
With strong inward desire to stray.

As the clouds of my bad decisions
Ominously gather above my head,
The storms of judgment organize
And shower my heart with dread.

Through the darkness of rebellion
I can see His light filling my space,
But inside of that light—a shadow,
The merciful shadow of His grace.

Falling down across my shoulders,
Totally covering my life all around,
Mysterious to me in all its meaning,
Because by sin I have been bound.

When I turn and face His presence
I recognize the antidote for my loss.
The graceful shadow that has fallen
Is clearly in the shape of the cross.

Who would have thought of grace
And the shadow that it might cast?

One shaped like Calvary's cross,
Cleansing all the faults of my past.

Cast the great shadow of Your grace
Upon my life, Lord, again and again.
For this old heart is my great enemy,
And all too often it tempts me to sin.

Let the Son shine down on your life
With the shadow of the cross in place,
His forgiveness as an eternal covering:
The wonderful shadow of His grace!

Psalm 91:1-2 He that dwelleth in the secret place of the most High shall abide under the shadow of the Almighty. I will say of the LORD, He is my refuge and my fortress: my God; in him will I trust.

Thoughts of the Heart

The Mist

If you are looking for answers to your questions of life, then God's word should be your source. It is there you will find the answers to your questions.

I see, though vaguely, into the mist.
Shapes and sounds and movements,
Interactions in the time and space
Mysteriously veiled in uncertainty.
Friends journey through the scene.

Incidents and events somewhat hidden—
A temporal fog enshrouds the details.
My mind attempts to weave together
Flaxen threads of meaning in it all;
Patterns of understanding are elusive.

Then through the vapor there emerges
An empyreal image above all the rest,
Eternally solid and foundational.
Calling out in the midst of the clamor,
"I alone am the searched-for truth.

"I live out beyond this mortal mist
Where the dwellers of earth cannot go
Until their time to leave the valley.
I have dwelt in the land for a season
And have paid the debt of the choices."

While traveling along my allotted path
I have determined to discover Him
And the peace His presence guarantees
My heart has invented all the questions
His response—to provide the answers.

Psalm 27:7-8 Hear, O LORD, when I cry with my voice: have mercy also upon me, and answer me. When thou saidst, Seek ye my face; my heart said unto thee, Thy face, LORD, will I seek.

The Fool Inside

One day we will no longer be subjected to our mortal self that loves to sin. Until then, we must depend on the Spirit of God as He illuminates His word and our minds.

Life, for me, is a considerable enigma
Because I share my mind with a fool
Whose opinions are constantly voiced
In the debate as to just who will rule.

My new life in Jesus Christ is blessed
With thoughts that center on the Word,
But I can always depend on that fool
To interrupt with ideas that are absurd.

One time I thought the fool was dead.
I soon realized he was not even sick.
When it comes to deceiving my heart
He is proficient at every subtle trick.

Until the day my flesh is gone forever
That old fool will make himself heard,
But he can be defeated by a daily dose
Of the truth found within God's word.

Psalms 119:11 Thy word have I hid in mine heart, that I might not sin against thee.

Before It Melts

Life is not simply a seemingly endless series of things that the Christian cannot do. It is so much more than that. If lived by God's grace, life becomes an endless series of situations that display what an awesome God we serve. There is joy upon joy that others, who do not know the Lord and His forgiveness, cannot know.

I got a large ice cream cone
At a counter the other day.
I knew the need to eat quickly
To keep it from melting away.

Spinning it from side to side
Carefully working it all around,
I didn't allow any to be wasted
By dripping onto the ground.

I faithfully stayed on guard
As the cone began to shrink,
Enjoying every single minute.
That's when I started to think.

If I should fail to stay involved
I'll be the one that will lose.
Ice cream was made to be eaten
And by its special taste, amuse.

Life is like that simple cone—
An opportunity limited by time—
Whether vanilla or strawberry
Or perhaps even lemon and lime.

We must stay spiritually active
To enjoy the taste each day
By giving the Lord first place—
Not letting life just melt away.

Work your way through them—
All the events that come and go.
Live them within God's grace.
Don't fret over what you don't know.

One day when you reach the end,
If by grace you have done it right,
You won't have wasted a single drop
Or missed out on a single bite.

Colossians 3:23 And whatsoever ye do, do it heartily, as to the Lord, and not unto men;

Decisions

A man once said that we have the freedom to make choices, but we do not have freedom to choose the consequences. Those little decisions to investigate things we know are not pleasing to God are seeds that grow up into a harvest of sorrow. Isn't it great to know that our Heavenly Father is ever willing to forgive our missteps and rescue us from our own bad choices. Many can testify to God's deliverance from the clutches of sin and the prisons where we resided. Most of the resulting scars are for our eyes only as reminders of God's mercy and grace, and our sinful choices.

Twas only a simple little thing—
The choice that came my way.
I mulled it all over in my mind,
Not sure just what I would say.

I had heard the details about it
And knew what authorities said,
But I made the decision anyway.
Just once, what is there to dread?

A single insignificant surrender
To a disease that God calls sin,
Drove an infection of the heart
To undiscovered depths within.

That first choice led to the second.
It appears that I had opened a door.
Just one taste of the forbidden fruit
Had created a deep desire for more.

My first step quickened into a trot,
And then my pace changed to a run.

The consequences became invoices,
Demanding payment for things done.

One day I looked up from my sin,
Found myself in bondage complete,
Desiring to withdraw from the pain,
I soon realized there was no retreat.

I had built stone walls all around me
With window bars made out of my sin.
Bad choices had constructed a prison,
And poor decisions had locked me in.

My mind searched for the answers—
The causes of my situation that day.
I wondered how life would have been
Had I instead done things God's way.

Now I muse, "Where can I go now?"
Life as a prisoner saddens my heart
With regrets about that first decision
If only I could go back to the start

A call sounds out from deep inside,
"Prison walls can be broken by grace."
Repent—asking God to cleanse you.
And bondage with freedom replace.

Psalm 40:1-3 I waited patiently for the LORD; and he inclined unto me, and heard my cry. He brought me up also out of an horrible pit, out of the miry clay, and set my feet upon a rock, and established my goings. and he hath put a new song in my mouth, even praise unto our God: many shall see it, and fear, and shall trust in the LORD.

Emotions

When personal tragedy and the emotional storm that it brings, enters your life, it can be simply overwhelming. Sorrow seems to crash over our lives like the waves of the ocean upon one standing in the shallows. Just about the time you feel you have gotten through the worst of it, another wave comes crashing down. As time passes, these waves of emotion usually come with less frequency and intensity. Will these events ever cease completely? Not for someone who has truly experienced a heart breaking tragedy. Yet God's grace is always available when these sorrows threaten to cause us to lose focus on His eternal perspective. When earthly sorrows come, and they will, run to Him and He will give you peace.

Along picturesque seashores
Waves break from time to time,
Crashing upon majestic places
In an age-old melody sublime.

The pace of rhythmic crescendos
Is greatly affected by strong winds
Both during and after the storms
That the atmosphere often sends.

When personal storms of emotion
Plunder the needful peace we seek,
Crescendos of pain can overwhelm
Leaving the heart and knees weak.

Intense interactions with tragedy
Often fill our horizons with grief,
As tender, kindhearted platitudes
Provide almost negligible relief.

What we know to be our reality
Comes calling the very next day,
The sun comes up—life goes on—
We are thrown back into the fray.

God's grace is always provided
With the crashing of each swell,
And the emotions they can bring
When our minds choose to dwell.

Grace helps us cope in the heart
When emotions want to control.
Blessed with all spiritual benefits
We find serenity within the soul.

New storms are on the radar of life
While our mortality is yet His will.
Someday all earthly trials will end
With God's eternal, "Peace be still."

Isaiah 26:3 Thou wilt keep him in perfect peace, whose mind is stayed on thee: because he trusteth in thee.

Outside To His Side

Working with the homeless and often hopeless of this world is a very sobering thing. With the difficulties of life compounded by wrong choices, the future can appear very bleak. What a privilege it is to see the grace of God reach into some of these broken lives and bring about fundamental changes. It is good to consider just where we could be if someone had not introduced us to the grace of God that changed our destiny forever. It should send us into the praise and worship mode with truly grateful hearts.

With no place to call home
The streets are hard and cold.
Though years are not many
The body is feeling very old.

Wondering how I got here,
Various steps along the way,
The choices were all my own.
Failure follows me every day.

Then someone sent a message
Of love and a brand new start,
That begins in simple faith
And giving Jesus my heart.

Helping hands reach out to me—
They place love on display.
Teaching me about a new life
And guiding me in a new way.

Now the wandering has ended.
The Lord has become my friend.
Loneliness no longer applies.
He will walk with me to the end.

I now look back on my journey
Having Traveled from so far away,
Moving from outside to His side,
And that's where I plan to stay.

Luke 4:18 The Spirit of the Lord is upon me, because he hath anointed me to preach the gospel to the poor; he hath sent me to heal the brokenhearted, to preach deliverance to the captives, and recovering of sight to the blind, to set at liberty them that are bruised,

Pulling Up the Covers

Sometimes I just hate to hear that old alarm clock do its thing. At other times I have partially awakened on my own and am just waiting for it to sound off. A great influence on my response to the noise it makes is the time at which I got to sleep the night before. Although the snooze button can provide a few more moments of rest, in the end you must move out of that warm comfort zone and on to the day at hand.

When I heard that awful noise
I knew just what I had to do—
Time to arise and prepare for
The day that was brand new.

My hand reached for the button
And stilled that disturbing sound.
That's when I pulled Up the covers
Quickly tucking them all around.

I just don't think I can do it—
Face the dawning of the day.
It's safe and warm right here.
I truly wish that I could stay.

Hidden from all the problems
And the difficulties they bring,
By staying under these covers
I won't have to deal with a thing.

Imagine if I took my covers
With me as I walked the day,
To keep me safe and warm
From storms along the way.

That would appear a little silly
To those who crossed my path.
Some would be quite concerned,
And others would simply laugh.

Well, you know the real truth.
We can't run and hide from life.
Sometimes things are smooth,
Other times filled with strife.

I know I must leave this comfort.
My God's covering is all I need.
Jesus, pull up the covers of my life—
The covers of Your grace indeed!

Isaiah 61:10 I will greatly rejoice in the LORD, my soul shall be joyful in my God; for he hath clothed me with the garments of salvation, he hath covered me with the robe of righteousness, as a bridegroom decketh himself with ornaments, and as a bride adorneth herself with her jewels.

Runs With Scissors

I recently heard about a progress report sent home by a kindergarten teacher that container the following phrase; "runs with scissors". Apparently this report referred to a young student who had been warned about the danger of running with scissors in his hand, and had repeatedly ignored the admonitions of his concerned teacher.

This school safety situation caused me to consider spiritual issues. It could have been said of me, in my younger years; "runs with scissors, plays with matches, rides in the street, explores storm drains," etc. I remember well the warnings, the discipline and the scars that came my way when I chose to do stupid and dangerous things, as a kid.

Sometimes now that we are grown up and matured physically and spiritually, we find ourselves once again "running with scissors". That phrase means engaging in potentially dangerous actions with common things of life that have a risk factor. Everyday things when used properly can be helpful, but when used in the wrong way or when we get in a rush, harmful results can occur.

I wonder if God has made a note on your record and mine that says; "he tends to run with scissors, but I've got him covered by My grace". Perhaps your scissors thing is; getting too busy to spend time in the word, or getting too interested in the business of others, or perhaps allowing the world to set up wrong priorities in your life. Remember that grace covers the problems caused when we spiritually run with scissors, but Godly wisdom would advise us not to run in the first place.

Lord teach us to live so that You can write on our account; "used to run with scissors, but now walks by grace". Isn't God's grace a wonderful thing?!

The Valentine

Telling the special people in our lives that we love them is always the right thing to do and Valentine's Day is a good time to do it. God has loved us and given us a new heart and a new future. Let's not forget to tell Him that we love Him.

I remember many years ago
As our teacher led the way,
We cut, trimmed, and pasted
A heart for Valentine's Day.

Bordered with colorful glitter
In shades of almost every hue
With a message printed across:
"You're very special, I love you."

They were not very well done.
Just a little messy, like kids do,
But the words they sent to Moms
Displayed all our feelings true.

Later on when life was changing
And we spotted that special one,
A candy filled heart was bought
And a bouquet kissed by the sun.

As love proceeds over the years,
Sometimes we forget to show
To the ones we love so dearly,
A truth that they already know.

This is a time now to remember
That they love to hear once again
These words: "I truly love you,
And cherish you deeply within!"

This reminds me of my Savior
Who died that I might be free,
And bought my eternal pardon
That sacrificial day at Calvary.

When I first gave Him my heart,
All tattered and stained by my sin,
He received it with tender love.
A new relationship we did begin.

Jesus is the King of Heart Repairs.
He puts the pieces back in place
Then fixes its rips and wrinkles,
Trimming it in mercy and grace.

Just give your life to Jesus daily.
Let His perfect love lead the way.
When you offer Him a loving heart
Every day will be Valentine's Day.

Psalm 147:3 He healeth the broken in heart, and bindeth up their wounds.

The Path

Jesus did not come as a great teacher giving directions to mankind to help them find some enlightened path. What He said was, "I am the path, and the only way to find God." Jesus and the Father are one, so when you get Jesus, you get it all.

I used to walk in the woods
Along a rarely traveled route,
With twists and turns familiar
That led me back round about.

Knowing the way extremely well
I was comfortable at all hours,
Never fearing to become lost
When distracted by wild flowers.

My guests enjoyed the adventure
When they joined me on my walk,
But they stayed close to the guide.
As we traveled they would talk.

"We've never been this way before.
We are glad we can walk with you"
As we move from place to place
Taking the direction that is true.

When I consider eternal things
And the place where we will be,
There is a path to be traveled
When from earth we are set free.

It leads to a place I've never been
On a path that I have never trod.
If only I could be provided a guide
To take me to the home of God.

Jesus came to show me the way.
In fact, He said that He was it,
And if I would believe in Him
In Heaven one day I would sit.

I've never been this way before
So I ask, "Can I walk with You?
I'll try to walk in Your steps
And do all the things You do.

And, oh, by the way, if You please,
I have one more urgent request.
There is a friend I'm thinking of.
Can he come along as a guest?

He has never been this way before,
And he needs Your guidance too.
Perhaps there might be some others.
Could be several or just a few.

Thank you for showing the way
That leads us out of the wrath.
I am so glad that You desired
To make Yourself the path."

John 14:6 Jesus saith unto him, I am the way, the truth, and the life: no man cometh unto the Father, but by me.

The Problem

It is necessary that we discuss possible solutions for problems that occur in our lives and seek good counsel. Yet sometimes these discussions will drag on and on, ad nauseam, and never reach any solutions. I see this occurring with leadership bodies like the United Nations, or the United States Congress, or even with our local governments. These organizations don't understand the blessing of submitting problems to God and allowing His grace to lead to the best solutions.

We often chew the gum of a problem
Until all the flavor is gone and then
Stick it in our hair or throw it down
For someone else to blindly step in.

We analyze, visualize, and synthesize,
Yet there is still a problem to be solved,
And in finding the permanent solution
Please remember grace will be involved.

Write it all down and turn it all around,
Then submit the whole thing in prayer.
Recognize that you need heavenly help:
God and His grace will meet you there.

You will have an important part to play
So be sure that you roll up each sleeve.
When God and grace and you team up—
The problem is solved, victory achieved.

Hebrews 4:16 Let us therefore come boldly unto the throne of grace, that we may obtain mercy, and find grace to help in time of need.

Considerations

Burnt Pizza Evangelism

Heidi and Greg were working in their Hungry Howie's pizza store in Ypsilanti, Michigan on Labor Day weekend when two customers entered. One was a father who lived in the area, and the other was his son-in-law who had brought the family to Michigan for a visit. It wasn't a very busy time at the store so after the order was entered, Heidi began chatting-up her guests. If you knew Heidi, you would know how typical this is for her.

Heidi discovered that the dad was a born-again Christian, about the time the order should have been finished. When they should have had fresh pizza and been on their way, God had another plan. The new employee, who was supposed to process the order, had missed it. Embarrassed, Heidi apologized to the men, re-entered the order and decided to take advantage of the delay.

Heidi turned her attention to the son-in-law and asked him if he was also a believer. He responded that he did not go to church as often as he should. His answer raised some red flags in her mind. She rephrased her query and said, "I meant are you saved?" He avoided answering the question so she asked the dad where he went to church. As it so happened, he attended a church that was just a stones throw from the home of a friend of Heidi's who had been recently saved. This was the opening that Heidi had been looking for.

Heidi shared with them how her friend had called her at the store to find out where she could get a book to "bone up" on Christianity. This friend was planning to take her children to a special program at a local church and was afraid they might ask her a question about being a Christian. "Just give them your testimony," Heidi had advised. When her friend asked what a testimony was, Heidi used the opportunity to share her own personal testimony.

The two men listened intently as Heidi related how her friend had taken a general head knowledge about God and turned it into a heart relationship that day. Since then, several members of her friend's family have also made this life changing decision. As Heidi's story was continuing, she was interrupted by something that rarely happens. The pizzas for these men had bubbled up and literally stuck to the top of the oven. Another embarrassing delay!

Her husband Greg came to the rescue by rushing two more pizzas into the oven while Heidi apologized again and left the men alone for a few moments. When she returned with two new beautifully baked pizzas, she heard the younger man telling his father-in-law, "That's what I think happened to me. I got saved here (pointing to his head), and not here (pointing to his heart). Heidi chimed in with, "You can have a whole new life just like my friend does".

With that, she wished them well and they went on their way. Heidi later confided to Greg that she regretted not having gotten the phone number of the father-in-law so she could follow up later. She resigned herself to never knowing what happened after they had left. Then she received the call. The father-in-law called to thank her and inform her that his son-in-law had made a decision to trust Jesus Christ as his Savior, in the hours before he left to take his family back home to St. Louis.

Wow! Burnt pizza evangelism! God used a missed order and burnt pizza, two rare events at a top-rated pizza restaurant. He did this to allow time for the gospel to be given to a total stranger. Imagine what else He can do if we who know Him are willing to seize the opportunity and speak up. Isn't God's grace a wonderful thing?!

Unspoken

When the issues of life threaten to overwhelm our hearts and push us to the limits of our emotions, there is a place of comfort reserved in the presence of the Father. As our words fail in their ability to describe the burden, the Spirit reads the heart, and intercedes on our behalf in celestial phrases that we could never speak. Why would we ever hesitate to make use of this wonderful provision of God's praying grace?

I have heard great men at prayer—
Lofty words and formal phrases,
The power to speak so boldly
With reverence that truly amazes.

Just to listen to women pray—
What a blessing that stirs the soul
When they bow before the Lord
With His presence as their goal!

There are prayers for salvation,
And the healing of those in need,
Petitions for the soul of another
Who to the Savior we would lead.

Prayers of intercession are made
Amidst the circumstances of life
For the daily provisions needed
By the children, husband and wife.

There is one not yet mentioned—
A special prayer that stands apart,

One that has no speech involved—
The silent prayer of a broken heart.

It is presented to God by a Person,
The Holy Spirit Who resides within,
When the senses are overwhelmed
And we don't know where to begin.

The language of our flesh fails us
As words become a tearful moan.
The Spirit reads the burdened heart
And intercedes for us with a groan.

Translating our unspoken thoughts,
Turning weeping to a grand appeal,
That moves the heart of the Father
In whose holy presence we kneel.

Rom. 8:26&27 Likewise the Spirit also helpeth our infirmities: for we know not what we should pray for as we ought: but the Spirit itself maketh intercession for us with groanings which cannot be uttered. And He that searcheth the hearts knoweth what is the mind of the Spirit, because He maketh intercession for the saints according to His purpose.

Kyle's Puzzle

I recently had the opportunity to watch a thirteen-year-old boy named Kyle work on a jigsaw puzzle. The pieces of the puzzle were a little larger than the ones that I enjoy doing, but that is completely understandable. Kyle is a severely mentally impaired teenager, suffers from seizures, and as a result has poor motor skills.

If you were to meet Kyle, his problems would be immediately obvious; yet there he was, successfully taking individual pieces, finding their place within the puzzle, matching the notches, and gradually making the fragmented picture whole again. Life, in general, has certainly not been easy for Kyle and his family as they lovingly work to put the pieces of his life together to help him be all that he can be in spite of many difficulties.

God has a plan for Kyle, as He has a plan for each of us. God's plan is for us to become a picture of His grace that is developed over the days of life that He ordains. If we surrender all the pieces to Him, He will fit each one together for His special purpose and create a beautiful scene for all to appreciate.

The picture of Kyle's life will not portray all the opportunities that some lives have, but that is not a problem. Kyle handles all his difficulties with patience while almost never complaining. He merely accepts whatever the day brings. He has become a neon display of God's providence and love for one who could be described as a weaker vessel. Weaker, perhaps, but less valuable—never!

The God of Heaven is a Master at using the weak things of this world to bring glory to Himself. After all, He chose us to be His children. And as the Apostle Paul said, "…when I am weak, then I am strong." In thinking about Kyle and his puzzle, I remember that God answered Paul's plea for healing with the words, "My grace is sufficient for thee; for my strength is made perfect in weakness." That advice is for all of us, including Kyle.

As I consider the puzzle that has been my life, and some of the mismatched pieces that I have vainly tried to fit together, I wonder how God perceives it all. When He sees Kyle and me standing together, I wonder which of us He considers being "the weaker vessel"? I dare say that there might be many who would not fare well in that type of comparison.

Hang in there, Kyle! One day your God will make all things new as we shed our earthly vessels of weakness for eternal robes of perfection in Jesus Christ. Your parents look forward to that heavenly day when they can have a long conversation with you, and together you can say, "Isn't God's grace a wonderful thing?"

Hey, what happened to that last piece of straight edge? It was here a minute ago. You don't suppose Kyle is hiding it so he can put the last touch on the puzzle do you? Nah, he wouldn't do that—would he?

The Puzzle

It is easy to get focused on the individual events and issues of our lives and lose sight of the big picture. Do you remember speaking with your children about making choices that seemed short sighted. God knows about the big picture for our lives because he designed us. We need to let Him help us build a life that reflects the things that He sees as important.

The picture was very beautiful
Gracing the outside of the box—
The clouds and heavens above,
The water, the ships, the rocks.

Inside things were very different.
There were pieces of every shape
That when properly put together
Will present a lovely landscape.

A machine had taken the image
Then precisely cut each tiny bit,
With straight edges and notches,
Each one needing the perfect fit.

Then the piecing process begins
As one by one the parts are wed,
Matching color, notch and edge,
Just as quickly as the eye is led.

Slowly the amalgam emerges.
Individual images become one.
Sections are partnered together,
And the puzzle is finally done.

Our lives just like a great puzzle
Are pieced together day by day—
Different parts at different times
In colors from turquoise to gray.

Looking at each individual piece
The appearance does not inspire.
Being appropriately fit together
Is all that your God will require.

He guides every step of the way
In the life which belongs to Him.
Parts that were once all scattered,
With His help begin looking trim.

Let the Master builder construct
The pieces into a beautiful whole,
Unified in God's graceful purpose
And complete, under His control.

Ephesians 2:19-22 Now therefore ye are no more strangers and foreigners, but fellowcitizens with the saints, and of the household of God; and are built upon the foundation of the apostles and prophets, Jesus Christ himself being the chief corner stone; in whom all the building fitly framed together groweth unto an holy temple in the Lord: in whom ye also are builded together for an habitation of God through the Spirit.

Lifted Above

How blessed it is to consider how God, by His mercy and grace, has lifted our hearts and lives and set us on the Solid Rock through our Lord and Savior, Jesus Christ.

I heard about a man who had waited patiently
For God to hear his cry and set his heart free.
He was hopelessly entrapped in a horrible pit
And longed for God's Rock upon which to sit.

This is what I desire, a change in my direction.
I need Your great love to make the correction.
I'll trade You this mess for a brand new start.
Lord, impart a new song deep within my heart.

Now Your grace and mercy have filled my soul.
Through Your suffering, I have been made whole.
You bought for me all the glories of eternity,
And through Your love, I have been set free.

Lord, now I'll follow, and now I'll run.
I'll glorify You for all that You have done
And with my life, I'll show that I'm in love,
For by Your blood, You've lifted me above.

Psalm 40:1-3 I waited patiently for the Lord; and he inclined unto me, and heard my cry. He brought me up also out of a horrible pit, out of the miry clay, and set my feet upon a rock, and established my goings. And he hath put a new song in my mouth, even praise unto our God: many shall see it, and shall trust in the Lord.

My Jilted Friend

If there is a period of silence between you and your heavenly Father, it always indicates a problem. Either your fellowship is not genuine or something has come between the two parties. This interruption of communication can be caused by some of the mundane things of life that at times dominate our schedule or more serious matters of sin. If you find yourself in this situation, purpose today to re-establish regular communication and allow His grace to repair your broken fellowship.

I have a very special Friend
Who has meant the world to me,
A loyal and wonderful Friend
Faithful to the last degree.

We have spent time together
Discussing my deepest fears,
Sharing the inside things—
Hopes and dreams and tears.

He called me just the other day.
It seems we had not talked,
And our relationship of sharing,
Away from it I had walked.

My silence was an obvious sign
That something had come between.
When I didn't return His call
A problem was clearly seen.

His heart was very disturbed
When I just didn't have the time
To talk to my dear old Friend
And express this heart of mine.

I had jilted my special Friend,
Yet that was never my plan.
Things had gotten in the way
As one day into another ran.

The struggles of life are legion,
The storms seem never to end.
My heart is heavily burdened.
I really miss my special friend!

I made a new contact yesterday
In hopes He would take my call.
His response was very welcome.
"Let's meet and talk about it all."

I had forsaken this dear Friend
Who had done so much for me.
And when I came to my senses
He was where I thought He'd be.

He was waiting for His friend
To share the truth of His heart,
Touching the inside of my life
In the grace of a brand new start.

Gen. 3:8 And they heard the voice of the LORD God walking in the garden in the cool of the day: and Adam and his wife hid themselves from the presence of the LORD God amongst the trees of the garden.

Search and Rescue

There is a True Shepherd who seeks to rescue wandering sheep. The ones that have been found and forgiven, must always remember the feeling of being lost and defeated. Too often an unforgiving spirit demands justice for the failures of others when grace has been freely dispensed to cover our foolishness and rebellion. After we have thanked Him and praised Him for our personal rescues, wouldn't it be a wonderful thing if we could become a part of the True Shepherd's search and rescue team?

If I were God I would lock the gate
When my sheep went through to leave,
And when they came back for mercy
There would certainly be no reprieve.

How foolish for them to exchange
The safety of remaining in the fold
For the fields of this present world
Where the heart is so cheaply sold.

I know that far pastures look green,
Where a fleshly feast is being served,
But adverse digestive consequences
Are a sad fate they so justly deserve.

I would allow their abuse to continue
For the foolishness that they embrace.
But thank goodness that God is not me.
His response is seasoned with grace.

Though many sheep remain inside
He still leaves the sheepcote behind,
And searches for that one who is lost,
With a spiritual restoration in mind.

When that stray is finally located,
Devastated by the ugliness of his sin,
He binds the wounds with forgiveness,
Reunited by His love and mercy again.

He picks up the one He has tended—
Strong arms hold him near to His heart,
And He bears him home from a journey
That would have been best not to start.

What a wonderful and loving Shepherd
Who not only has prepared us a place,
But seeks after the fool in his folly
And restores him with forgiving grace!

Luke 19:10 For the Son of man is come to seek and to save that which was lost.

The Idea

Writers of any size shape or level of skill, I wrote the following just for you. Mind you that the principle involved has been the nemesis of writers throughout recorded history. Some have written masterpieces that inspire us thousands of years later; some have written crude passages that are barely usable for informational or research purposes; and many others have simply missed wonderful opportunities when they found other things to be more important. Communicating with the written word and the verbal presentations that often follow is a work that is empowered by inspiration, and accomplished by determination. How sad it is to be presented in your spirit with a wonderful and creative thought, and fail to take the time to record that precious idea for future development. After bemoaning this fact in conversation with a fellow writer, I purposed to limit my loses in this area, by taking the time necessary to—WRITE IT DOWN!

A thought came into my mind,
Seems just only a moment ago.
I knew I should write it down,
But—too busy—I just said, "no."

It was a very unique idea
Filled with wonderful possibilities
To be explored and considered
When my schedule is more at ease.

I'll just consider it in my mind,
And enjoy all the ins and outs,
Then trust it all to memory,
And come back later no doubt.

Then something not strange occurred
When I went to find my treasure,
To dig it up with enthusiasm,
And to handle it with pleasure.

I could not find it anywhere—
Yet yesterday it was so clear!
I searched and looked diligently,
But that idea just wasn't there.

I am positive it was a great one
Yes, a Pulitzer prize perhaps,
But there I was empty minded
This old brain just had a lapse.

I need to give you a warning,
I think you know my plight.
Ideas are meant to be recorded,
Before they go clean out of sight.

When you get a fantastic idea,
Write down that burning ember.
If you put it off until later,
You probably won't remember.

Author—write it down!
Pastor—write yourself a note!
Poet—frame it out!
Songwriter—do the chords!

Talents

In the growing up years, there are times when the kids choose up sides for a game. This can be a truly difficult time for the child who so desperately wishes to be selected, but has little to offer his teammates in the area of physical dexterity. He waits as the team captains rotate in selection of player after player, while carefully avoiding the disadvantage of choosing those individuals whose limitations will hurt a winning effort. What a blessing it is when a talented, but also sensitive, captain purposely chooses the unwanted player early in the selection process and later sees to it that this weaker link truly feels a part of the team. We need to teach children that God has gifted each of us differently and when they are strong at a particular activity they must keep an eye out for those who struggle in their area of strength. Compassion for others, in these situations, is so much more important than the outcome of the game.

I remember this one little boy,
Not much at the jump and run.
He was always the last chosen
When the choosing was done.

Not gifted with speed of foot,
Less than athletically inclined,
For any physical competition
He was certainly not designed.

Oh, how he hated those times
When the games must be played.
His weaknesses demonstrated
And lack of ability displayed.

Then one day it just happened.
He had thought it never could.
Algebra and hard stuff like that—
He could do it and do it good!

Other things began to develop
That he was very good at, too.
When the old gang needed help
He knew precisely what to do.

He didn't remind them how they
Had mocked, and teased and hurt,
And how many times he had hidden
A broken heart beneath his shirt.

You may know someone like this
Whose talents have not yet shown,
Never observed before in public
And to extremely few are known.

Wait patiently for them to bloom.
Love them for who they really are.
Watch as God blesses their talent
And then develops them into a star.

Romans 12:10 Be kindly affectioned one to another with brotherly love; in honor preferring one another;

The Last Flight

My father was a pilot in the United States Air Force during WWII and served in Asia flying a C-46 over the Himalayan Mountains in a region known as the Hump. Although it has been over sixty years since that time, I still consider him a soldier. This is dedicated to him and all those who fought with him to defend this great nation.

They came from every direction
From families large and small.
They launched out on a mission
And answered their nation's call.

They flew on wings made of steel,
And the dangers of war they faced.
Strong hands controlled their craft
As those powerful engines raced.

In time the great conflict was won
Although costing a terrible price,
As too many members of the band
Made life's ultimate sacrifice.

Now time has become the enemy.
Years have so quickly passed by,
Witnessed by losses in the ranks
Of that old gang that used to fly.

Yet in the minds of all who remain,
Keen remembrance of days before,
When they took great metal birds
And through the clouds did soar.

There is one very special mission
All old pilots are required to take.
The call comes from Headquarters.
It's a flight that we all must make.

This one last flight is like no other,
For our God has planned the way.
He alone will determine the place
And choose the time and the day.

When Operations sends out the call
Those pilots who have sailed on air,
Will take their last earthly flight,
To a place that God has prepared.

Dedicated to the members of the Hump Pilot's Association and American aviators everywhere.
Rev. Cook is the son of Floyd T. Cook, pilot, 12th ComCar Sq. 3rd Gp. Myitkyina, Burma

The Visit

When people visit our house, you can be sure that everything is in order and clean, due to the many hours of work that preceded the appointed date. With the Lord, things are different. He desires to visit us everyday and do all the cleaning Himself. If you open the door, He will make your life clean and fresh.

When someone special comes to visit our humble abode
A scramble of activity precedes: in cleaning, all share a load.
We desire to present our home in its best possible light,
Dusting and mopping every corner, making it look just right.

There are times when a dignitary plans a visit to our home town.
The clean-up starts in earnest and things get fixed-up all around.
Whether presidents or kings, we want to show them our best
With everything in its place and the children properly dressed.

There is One greater than all, Who desires to visit each day,
But when He arrives at our door, too often we turn Him away.
We think our space isn't ready for a visit from Heaven's King.
The dust and dirt of this world is covering almost everything.

What makes our Master unique are the steps He is willing to take
To place our lives in order and all the needed corrections make.
He is willing to do all the work so put your sincere efforts away.
Welcome His visit within your heart; He will make you clean today.

Ephesians 5:25-27 Husbands, love your wives, even as Christ also loved the church, and gave himself for it; that he might sanctify and cleanse it with the washing of water by the word, that he might present it to himself a glorious church, not having spot, or wrinkle, or any such thing; but that it should be holy and without blemish.

INDEX

LaVergne, TN USA
02 March 2010

174371LV00004B/2/P